Martin Knura

Companies and Environmental Impact

Identification and Visualization
of Key Ecological Indicators

Diplomica® Verlag GmbH

Knura, Martin: Companies and Environmental Impact: Identification and Visualization of Key Ecological Indicators. Hamburg, Diplomica Verlag GmbH 2013

ISBN: 978-3-8428-7989-8
Druck: Diplomica® Verlag GmbH, Hamburg, 2013

Bibliografische Information der Deutschen Nationalbibliothek:
Die Deutsche Nationalbibliothek verzeichnet diese Publikation in der Deutschen Nationalbibliografie; detaillierte bibliografische Daten sind im Internet über http://dnb.d-nb.de abrufbar.

Die digitale Ausgabe (eBook-Ausgabe) dieses Titels trägt die ISBN 978-3-8428-2989-3 und kann über den Handel oder den Verlag bezogen werden.

Dieses Werk ist urheberrechtlich geschützt. Die dadurch begründeten Rechte, insbesondere die der Übersetzung, des Nachdrucks, des Vortrags, der Entnahme von Abbildungen und Tabellen, der Funksendung, der Mikroverfilmung oder der Vervielfältigung auf anderen Wegen und der Speicherung in Datenverarbeitungsanlagen, bleiben, auch bei nur auszugsweiser Verwertung, vorbehalten. Eine Vervielfältigung dieses Werkes oder von Teilen dieses Werkes ist auch im Einzelfall nur in den Grenzen der gesetzlichen Bestimmungen des Urheberrechtsgesetzes der Bundesrepublik Deutschland in der jeweils geltenden Fassung zulässig. Sie ist grundsätzlich vergütungspflichtig. Zuwiderhandlungen unterliegen den Strafbestimmungen des Urheberrechtes.

Die Wiedergabe von Gebrauchsnamen, Handelsnamen, Warenbezeichnungen usw. in diesem Werk berechtigt auch ohne besondere Kennzeichnung nicht zu der Annahme, dass solche Namen im Sinne der Warenzeichen- und Markenschutz-Gesetzgebung als frei zu betrachten wären und daher von jedermann benutzt werden dürften.

Die Informationen in diesem Werk wurden mit Sorgfalt erarbeitet. Dennoch können Fehler nicht vollständig ausgeschlossen werden, und der Diplomica Verlag, die Autoren oder Übersetzer übernehmen keine juristische Verantwortung oder irgendeine Haftung für evtl. verbliebene fehlerhafte Angaben und deren Folgen.

© Diplomica Verlag GmbH
http://www.diplomica-verlag.de, Hamburg 2013
Printed in Germany

Table of Contents

List of abbreviations III

Register of Illustrations... IV

1. Introduction 1

2. Ecology and Sustainability – How does this relate? 7

2.1 What is sustainability?...7

2.2 Placement of ecology 11

2.3 Functions of nature 13

2.4 Health of nature 18

3. Key Ecological Indicators 21

3.1 What are KEIs?..21

3.2 Requirements for KEIs 28

3.3 Classification of KEIs 31

3.4 Positioning and usage of KEIs 34

3.4.1 Macro-view 34

3.4.2 Micro-view 36

3.5 Determination of KEIs..45

4. Building a KEI Framework for Business-Processes 55

4.1 Introducing the Case study..56

4.2 Defining properties of the KEI Framework...58

4.3 Selection of processes-based KEIs..60

4.4 Architecture 64

4.4.1 Monitoring of process-execution... 66

4.4.2 Measurement of substances and energies... 68

4.4.3	Granularity of data		79
4.4.4	Datawarehouse Design		80
4.4.5	Extract Transform Load Process		93
4.4.6	Aggregation of data and calculation of KEIs		100
4.4.7	Visualization of KEIs		102
5.	Conclusion		107
6.	Outlook		111
7.	References		VII

List of abbreviations

API	Application Programming Interface
B-to-B	Business-to-Business
B-to-C	Business-to-Consumer
BPEL	Business Process Execution Language
BPM	Business Process Management
BPMN	Business Process Modeling Notation
CEP	Complex Event Processing
DW	Datawarehouse
EIS	Environmental Information System
EM	Environmental Management
EMS	Environmental Management System
EPA	Environmental Protection Agency
ERM	Entity-Relationship Model
ESOR	Environmentally Sustainable Online Reseller (company name)
ETL	Extract Transform Load
KEI	Key Ecological Indicator
KEIs	Key Ecological Indicators
KPI	Key Performance Indicator
KPIs	Key Performance Indicators
ODE	Orchestration Directory Engine
ODS	Operational Data Store
SLA	Service Level Agreement
SLAs	Service Level Agreements

Register of Illustrations

Figure 1 - Aims of this work 5
Figure 2 - Perspective on the systems 12
Figure 3 - Linear throughput depiction of the socio-economic process 15
Figure 4 - Process Interfaces 17
Figure 5 - Correlation of Indicators 28
Figure 6 - Different Environmental indicators 32
Figure 7 - Classification of KEIs 33
Figure 8 - BPM Lifecycle 38
Figure 9 - Components of an EMS 39
Figure 10 - Modules of Eco Accounting 41
Figure 11 - Derivation of KEIs 47
Figure 12 - BPMN Diagram of the underlying business-process 58
Figure 13 - Extract of ESORs Strategy 61
Figure 14 - General Architecture for KEI aware process execution 65
Figure 15 - Sequence Diagram - Event Capturing 66
Figure 16 - Class diagram of defined Events for EventManager 68
Figure 17 - Class Diagram EcoSimulator 71
Figure 18 - ConfigManager File 75
Figure 19 - Functioning of EventManager simulating energy data 77
Figure 20 - Sequence Diagram EventManager 78
Figure 21 - Datawarehouse ERM 82
Figure 22 - Relationship Schema 83
Figure 23 - Table Substance Type 86
Figure 24 - Table Substance 87
Figure 25 - Table Energy Mix 88
Figure 26 - Table Indicator Types 89
Figure 27 - Table Indicator Level 90
Figure 28 - Table Indicator Definition 91
Figure 29 - Table Indicator Target 93
Figure 30 - Class diagram CEP Event 95

Figure 31 - Sequence Diagram ETL Process 97
Figure 32 - Class diagram - ETL and DWConnection 99
Figure 33 - Dashboard for ESOR – Overview 103
Figure 34 – Dashboard for ESOR – Activities 105

1. Introduction

Our planet with its life friendly environment is the foundation of our lives. Without it we and all living things wouldn't exist, so one could say it is the most important basis for our existence, and thus should be one of the most relevant subjects in our society. But if you face reality Mother Nature is exploited and destroyed by men and corporations for resources, money and profits, as could be seen in contemporary events, like the oil spill of the Deepwater Horizon in the Gulf of Mexico, or the nuclear disaster at the atomic plant in Fukushima. These events showed us, very obviously, how easy corporations could harm the vulnerable eco-system in a sustainable way. Moreover they pollute the environment with all their activities not only with serious accidents or scandals that are reported by the media, and thereby are in the awareness of a huge variety of people. Almost everything corporations do, more or less, will have an impact on our ecological system, as our own behavior will influence it as well.

In the last centuries though, more and more people began to question those reckless methods that violate our nature. They start to wonder how such an attitude would influence our future. Could it lead to an unlivable planet, so that following generations will not be able to live anymore? In deed this question targets a very pessimistic scenario, but is illustrating importance, as well as necessity of ecological health for humankind and all living creatures on planet earth. It is resulting in further questions, like which impact does our present behavior have on our environment, and how will it develop in the following years. Or in which way do we have to change our manner to ensure a healthy and livable environment in future. Additionally there are the so called "what if scenarios", which ask for instance, what environmental pollution would be if all developing countries behaved the way we do. As one can see, there are plenty of problems our society has to think about. Some of the biggest issues scientists have recognized are the greenhouse effect associated with the global warming problem, the limited amount of non-renewable resources like carbon, oil or gas, the urbanization of our planet and the shrinking biosphere for other creatures.[1] These issues show the need keeping track of our influence on Mother Nature and the urgency reducing it to a non-critical amount. Therefore the Environmental Protection Agency (EPA) has identified a huge potential for the economic sector reducing greenhouse gas emissions[2].

But what could motivate enterprises spending time, effort and money for environmental concerns? As it is a public good it is implying that the government should be responsible for that. Because of this statement it seems to be very obvious that businesses are not voluntarily interested in investing into public goods, which won't generate direct profits.[3] Nevertheless, more and more corporations consider a way improving their environmental impact and indeed every fifth manager sees the environment as a very important subject[4].

To explain such a divergence one can look at stakeholder theory. It assumes that not only shareholders will have an interest in a company, but also other groups like government or society. Their interests differ from the classical maximization of profits. As a consequence the environment might be of interest for stakeholders and therefore to organizations too, which will result in new objectives for corporations. In the end compromises of different interests must be made, revealing that more aspects than profit should matter.[5]

This explanation by stakeholder-theory has an implicit assumption, namely that improving environmental impact will cost money. Further it will come with a decrease of profits and will result in a conflict of interests. However several authors[6] argue that this must not be the case. But you could also improve your profits by becoming "greener", which would even encourage shareholders to become more ecofriendly. In short this concept is known under the term eco-efficiency. It means that one is trying to become more efficient by using fewer resources for the same outcome or in short "do more with less" and thus im-

---

[1] Cf. Kottmann, H., et al. (1999), p.21., Olson, E.G. (2009), p.8., Braun, B. (2002), p.1. and Hilgenkamp, K. (2006), p.12ff.
[2] Cf. Olson, E.G. (2009), p.9.
[3] Cf. Lesourd, J.B., Schilizzi, S.G.M. (2001), p.16.
[4] Cf. Buß, E. (2007), p.213.
[5] Cf. Lesourd, J.B., Schilizzi, S.G.M. (2001), p.5f.
[6] Cf. Braun, B. (2002), p.3. or DeSimone, L. D., et al. (1997), p.2.

proving environmental performance, as well as increasing profits. Therefore environmental protection might become a so called "win-win situation" or a strategic option that exposes to be an opportunity for enterprises to be better as their competitors and establish a good reputation by communicating their effort in reducing impact on Mother Nature.

Because of this awareness some companies claim that they actually care about the environment and advertise their eco-friendly products, processes or behavior, but cannot really prove their assertions. Parisi and Maraghini, for instance, detected that 90 percent of the biggest US-companies make promises about sustainability improvements and thereby also to the environment, but only 35 percent can actually prove that they observe their promises by measuring progress.[7] This might be one of the causes for the term "Greenwashing" that has come up in recent years. It is an expression for a marketing strategy, where "businesses try to make their practices look greener than they actually are"[8]. Such corporations, who takes environmental concerns, as well as corporate responsibility seriously, but not just wanting to improve their reputation in short-term, without really caring about the environment, must be able to prove their effort without having a "Greenwashing" marketing strategy.

These mentioned examples show that there are "multiple forces pushing enterprises to become better environmental stewards."[9] Olson tried to identify and structure those multiple forces by categorizing them into three tiers.[10] He started with foundational drivers, which are in fact the reason why ecological concerns emerge and thus are the big environmental problems that have to be solved. In this category he identified two significant problems: the global warming problem, related with climate and weather changes and the increasing demand of humanity that is caused by population growth and industrialization. These are the major causes for him, which "the world must learn to manage, to avoid adverse impacts on the environment and Earth's natural resources"[11]. These foundational drivers cause further impacts, inducing several risks again. As impacts of

---

[7] Cf. Parisi, C., Maraghini, M.P. (2010), p.131.
[8] Conner, N. (2009), p.286.
[9] Olson, E.G. (2009), p.7.
[10] Cf. ebenda (2009), p.7.
[11] Olson, E.G. (2009), p.8.

these foundational drivers he has identified "public pressure for environmental stewardship", "natural resources & raw material scarcity", "water stress" and "national security & safety concerns". Risks that are evolving from these impacts are "economic risks", "market risks", "regulatory risks", "reputational risks" and "operational & supply chain risks". So in fact all these mentioned impacts and risks are extrinsic motivations for corporations to become more eco-sensible. Of course the listed forces are not an entire enumeration of all conceivable forces and the earlier mentioned intrinsic motivation, named eco-efficiency has not been considered either, but it is still a first attempt to explain different motives and inducements for companies investing effort in improving environmental performance.

All preceding assertions exhibit that there are many extrinsic, as well as intrinsic motivations for the reasons why corporations should decrease their environmental impact. But how can corporations operationalize this objective and verifiably improve their environmental performance?

The phrase "if you measure it, you can manage it"[12] is giving one hint to that question. This is one opportunity where IT could support corporations. It enables an effective and efficient implementation of a measurement system, which can gather environmentally relevant information in an automatic or semi-automatic manner, calculate and aggregate them to indicators and visualize the results adjusted to relevant authorities. Based on these indicators, executives can make profound decisions, direct and optimize their company in a way that is environmental friendly, and in the end can ensure competitiveness, as well as long-term survival for their organization. They are further enabled to communicate and prove their environmental performance based on quantitative numbers and establish a good reputation in long-term, without using short-term "Greenwashing" marketing strategies.

After showing some examples for motivations, and relevance of IT-based environmental performance measurement to corporations, it comes to the purpose of this work, which is to identify and visualize Key Ecological Indicators. First some preparatory work is necessary to get all the theoretical information need-

---

[12] Zee, H. (2002), p.5.

ed. To achieve this goal it is further required identifying KEIs, establishing a measurement system to monitor environmental impact of a corporation, persisting the measured data and processing it to calculate the identified KEIs. The next step is developing a management dashboard to visualize selected KEIs in an appropriate way. The theoretical part of this work is actually considering environmental impact and KEIs from an overall corporation perspective, as it is needed to understand the context the practical work (Building a KEI framework for business-processes). So chapter 4 is limited to the business-process perspective being a subarea of the overall corporation perspective. Therefore the abovementioned steps will be executed for identifying and visualizing KEIs, highlighted green in Figure 1. Steps four "optimize processes" and five "control performance" are actually not part of this work, but are the logical consequences taking place next. Additionally there is an iterative component in this figure. A continuous improvement process should always be considered to become better and keep the system to the state of the art.

Thus the contributions of this work are developing theoretical foundations of KEIs and the implementation of a KEI framework for business-processes, exemplarily be done for a case study. By this case study, possibilities to calculate and visualize KEIs will be discussed.

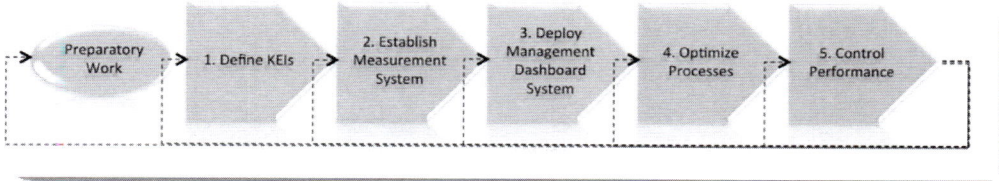

Figure 1 - Aims of this work[13]

---

[13] Refers to: Olson, E.G. (2009), p.89.

2. Ecology and Sustainability – How does this relate?

Starting with the basis for understanding environmental concerns by showing the relation of ecology to sustainability and vice versa, as it is indispensable for KEIs to be discussed. A general understanding of the term "sustainability" is needed, as well as an understanding of the perspective upon and the placement of ecology to determine priority of ecological aspects. Afterwards the fundamental functions and goods provided by nature will be discussed. It illustrates interfaces between economy and ecology, indicating where corporations and their business-processes affect nature. Finally conditions of environmental health will be discussed. It will show the relationship between ecology and sustainability, and will point out opportunities for corporations to contribute solving environmental problems.

2.1 What is sustainability?

Before the main chapter about Key Ecological Indicators commences it is necessary to talk about a very popular concept named sustainability, mentioned incidentally in the introduction of this work, and being absolutely fundamental for understanding ecological concerns and objectives. So the first preparatory work is answering the question: what does sustainability mean and really stand for?
Historically it possibly started in the 18th century where one of the main resources was wood. As the need for wood had increased people began to cut more wood. Soon they reached a state, as trees couldn't grow as fast as they were cut. It was probably the reason for the emergence of the first known sustainability thoughts. People recognized that it would be more effective cutting only such an amount of trees that can grow back in the same period of time, implying not to live on the substances itself, but on the revenues generated by it.[14]

---

[14] Cf. Grunwald, A., Kopfmüller, J. (2006), p.14.

This was a fundamental recognition that was very important for the future development of our ecological system, and shaped our understanding of the term sustainability. It implies a restriction for the use of the natural resource wood and thereby also restricts the economic activity for humankind that relies on this resource in short-term, but in long-term it guarantees relative constant revenues for all future generations. So one could say it is enabling all generations to cut the nearly same amount of wood.

After this historical excursion the next step to mention playing a major part in our understanding of sustainability was the famous Brundtland Report with its definition of sustainable development:

"Sustainable development is development that meets the needs of the present without compromising the ability of future generations to meet their own needs."[15]

In principal it abstracted the sustainable wood cutting notion into a more universal statement usable in almost every topic. Based on this understanding the previous constraint for woodcutting ensured that all generations will be able to satisfy their need for wood, as well as current generations not running out of it. The ability to use the term "sustainable development" very generally is caused by diplomatic language, and is the reason why this concept is criticized as to be too unspecific.[16] Thus the real question that this definition evolves is what "needs" do present and future generations have to specify what has to be done to ensure sustainable development. This philosophic question is indeed not easy to answer, and this work does not claim answering it, but some of the needs concerning nature will become clearer in section 2.3. Thereby the mentioned statements illustrate importance to concretize the definition of sustainability for different domains, because they will have a varying influence on the ability of current and future generations satisfying their needs. Additionally this specification will be needed to set realistic and practical objectives for corporations wanting to contribute to sustainable development. As this work is mostly concentrating on a business-specific view it is requisite considering what sus-

---

[15] Young, T., Burton, M.P. (1992), p.2.
[16] Cf. Sheldon, C., Yoxon, M. (2002), p.7.

tainability means in this context, which topics it includes, and how it can be operationalized. A very popular concept to differentiate various subjects of corporate sustainability is called the sustainability triangle. It contains three different dimensions named economy, ecology and society. These three points are the main areas and together build the business understanding of sustainability. It follows a short explanation for what those keywords stand for giving a better imagination what they mean.

The economic dimension ensures long-term survival, as well as competitiveness of a corporation. Thereby it considers the ecological and social dimension.[17]

The ecological dimension is about reducing environmental impact, which is induced by economic activities of corporations.[18]

Finally the social dimension considers impacts of economical acting to total society and especially includes a respectful handling of employees, good relationship to stakeholders, and responsibility towards society.[19]

So in fact corporations have to consider three different dimensions of needs that together will ensure sustainable existence of their organization, as well as supporting sustainable development for society. Corporations will need the social dimension, for example, for getting employees, customers, or social legitimacy for their economic activities. The ecological dimension will be needed to get resources and other services provided by nature, being discussed in section 2.3. Finally business will be there to make and earn money for an (ideally) infinite period of time, which are needs of the economic dimension. If one were missing the corporation would probably not exist and thus not be sustainable.

These different dimensions of course don't complement each other in each case. If, for instance, the ecological dimension was to be improved it could possibly come along with a decrease of the economic dimension by a more expensive, but environmental friendlier business-process. This example illustrates the big challenge that corporations are confronted with by sustainability. They have

---

[17] Cf. Hüttner (2001), p.47. and Küker (2003), p.31.
[18] Cf. Schaltegger, S., Dylilick, T. (2002), p.33.
[19] Cf. Wilkens, S. (2007), p.12ff.

to integrate[20] these different dimensions with their different objectives to a coherent concept so that all interests of their stakeholders and shareholders are considered and the final result of all dimensions will be maximized. The problem with this maximization is that especially progress to the social and ecological dimension are hardly appraisable with monetary numbers, so evaluating how much effort should actually be performed to those areas is hard. Besides the mentioned forces and motivations in the introduction there is another relevant subject named corporate responsibility that could give a hint determining the scope of effort. Corporations posses an important role in our society and influence our lives in many ways significantly. For example the prosperity of our society depends on the economy, as it creates jobs and income for their employees, or by paying taxes corporations can also support the whole society. But they have negative effects too by causing pollution, noise, or material scarcity. Because of these diverse effects they should consider expectations and values of society, as they need the social legitimacy for their existence.[21] Corporations that realized this mutual dependency feel responsible for their negative effects on society and ecology and therefore try keeping them as low as possible. This on the other hand could lead to an improved reputation, which today progressively determines the value of an enterprise.[22]

Integrating these three needs is a challenge that is tried to solve in corporations by sustainability management, and standards like ISO 26000[23] have evolved to support corporations with that challenge. In this work there will be a strong focus on the ecological dimension and its relation with the other systems and not on the integration and maximization of all three dimensions.

Moreover it raises a certain question: how could priority of the ecological dimension within corporations be derived? It is particular interesting for showing relevance of reducing environmental impact. The effort that is going to be performed to ecology might depend on the perspective upon and the priority of

---

[20] Cf. Schaltegger, S., et al. (2007), p.14ff.
[21] Cf. Gruber, K.A. (2009), p.71f.
[22] Cf. Buß, E. (2009), p.218.
[23] ISO 26000 (2011), URL see references

ecology that stakeholders, shareholders, management, and society possess, which will be considered in the following section.

2.2 Placement of ecology

It became clear that ecology does definitely relate to sustainability in some way, because it will be essential for life and will be one primary need of present and future generations. The introduced sustainability triangle assumes that all three dimensions should be, in some degree, equally important for corporations and have the same priority. But if reflecting about the common practices this will probably be not really the case.

To demonstrate how importance of each dimension could be derived and how ecology could be placed a model of Senge will be presented. He has tried to show two perspectives from which businesses or humanity could see the correlation of the three dimensions.

The left part of Figure 2 demonstrates the classical notion of how businesses see, and understand the hierarchy of these systems. It assumes that within economy, or also as a special case within one enterprise there are two smaller systems called ecology and society. In this way it implicitly has the assumption that profits are the most relevant aspect for economy respectively corporations and the remaining two systems are merely from secondary relevance. Thus they have not an equal importance as economic aspects when objectives for enterprises will be set. This perspective is stated as the exclusive eco-efficiency thought where these mentioned "secondary" systems are only considered, if not negatively affecting or even increasing the main goal realizing as much profits as possible. Such companies see the environment strictly as a public good that is entirely the responsibility of the government and not of themselves. Therefore they only observe regulations that law does make to environmental protection. But if this perspective should illustrate reality with the logical correlation of these systems and not from a very business-centric kind of view it would rather look like the right part of Figure 2 where ecology is the foundation of the other systems.

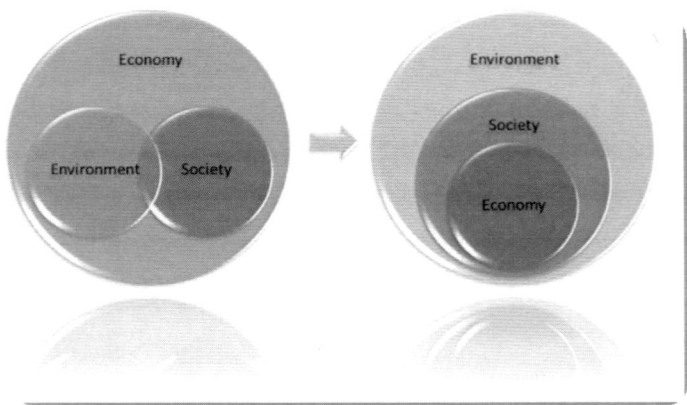

Figure 2 - Perspective on the systems[24]

It is a complete different perspective implying that in particular environmental objectives should have the highest priority to humanity and corporations. Of course this assumption conflicts with the purpose of economy to make money and profits. It is a very idealistic respectively theoretical point of view for the economic-sector, but it demonstrates that as the sustainability triangle assumes social and ecological objectives should have at least the same, or an approximately equal priority as economical ones. Corporations possessing this perspective realized and are aware of the responsibility they bear for ecology and society, thereby following the concept of corporate responsibility.

At last there is a certain aspect unmentioned illustrated in Figure 2. As has been shown in the introduction and section 2.1 there are multiple motivations inducing corporations to think about their environmental impact, which is represented as the arrow from the left to the right perspective, and clarifies the slowly changing perspective caused by these mentioned forces that corporations as well as humanity do have regarding environmental concerns, and yet provides another motivation for corporations reducing their environmental impact.

---

[24] Senge, P., et al. (2008), p.102.

2.3 Functions of nature

After showing priority of ecology it is necessary to take a closer look on nature itself. Especially before one can measure environmental impact of corporations to identify and calculate Key Ecological Indicators it is essential to recognize interfaces from environment to economy and vice versa. Which functions does Mother Nature provide for us in general and classify being observed to reduce impact of our economical acting and ensure environmental health.

In the preceding section Figure 2 illustrated the environment being the basis for all following systems and thus is the "initial source of all human endeavor"[25]. Wackernagel and Rees even intensify this statement by saying:

"We are not just connected to nature – we are nature. As we eat, drink and breathe, we constantly exchange energy and matter with our environment."[26]

These two sentences additionally show why nature is absolutely worth being protected, and really has to be preserved for future generations. In this statement there is also a note to a very general, but fundamental function that Mother Nature provides for us namely the exchange of energy and matter. We use and consume resources provided by our ecological system and cause emissions and wastes, which have to be absorbed by the ecosphere.[27] These goods and services that earths' ecological system performs to society are categorized into the areas "provisioning", "regulating", "supporting services" and "cultural & amenity"[28]. They will be concretized and illustrated by some examples giving a little perception for what those short keywords stand for.

With "provisioning" things like water & food, raw materials, fuel & energy, genetic resources, medical resources, and ornamental resources are meant.[29] It consequently contains all types of resources, renewable as well as non-renewable ones provided by nature, which are consumed by living creatures, plants and organizations. The category "regulating" means services like climate regulation, disturbance prevention, water regulation, soil retention, waste treat-

---

[25] Lawn, P. (2006), p.17.
[26] Wackernagel, M., Rees, W. (1996), p.7.
[27] Cf. Wackernagel, M., Rees, W. (1996), p.8.
[28] Cf. Groot, R., et al. (2006), p.227.
[29] Cf. ebenda, p.227.

ment and biological control[30], thus it has something to do with our ecological system absorbing wastes, emissions, and recycling these into new usable resources. "Supporting services" are for example habitat & refugium, biogeochemical cycles, soil formation, and nutrient regulation.[31] These services could be stated as location and soil services, which are not ultimately consumed, but used by humanity, living creatures, and plants. Moreover nature provides functions, summarized under the category "cultural & amenity", including aesthetic information, recreation and tourism, inspiration for art, folklore, spiritual information, historic information, science and education.[32] These are additional benefits that nature supplies for humanity.

Those examples illustrate how diverse and important the functions are that our ecological system does provide for us containing needs that humanity does and will have concerning nature, so that the question "what needs do current and future generations have?" raised by the definition of sustainable development is partially answered concerning needs to nature.

Following this, the identified goods and services will be refined for a more business-specific kind of view, and its relation to the other systems illustrated in Figure 3.

---

[30] Cf. ebenda, p.227.
[31] Cf. ebenda, p.227.
[32] Cf. ebenda, p.227.

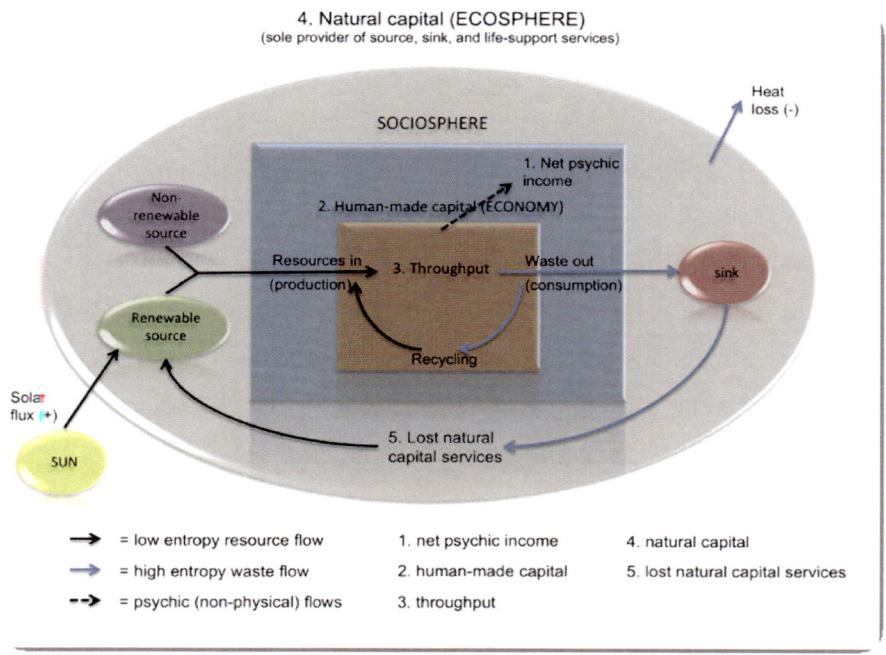

Figure 3 - Linear throughput depiction of the socio-economic process[33]

In this figure one can see the three foundational systems economy (orange), sociosphere (blue) and ecosphere (grey), which already came up in the preceding chapters and its detailed correlation with each other. Figure 3 contains the realistic hierarchy of systems introduced on the right part of Figure 2. Additionally it adds another relevant part being absolutely essential for the evolution of our earth, the sun. It provides solar energy for renewable resources like plants, for instance, which transfer carbon dioxide to oxygen by photosynthesis. The opposite of renewable resources are non-renewable resources. They are not naturally rebuilt and exist in a constraint amount implying they are not sustainable. These two kinds of resources together are provided by the provisioning function of ecosphere and used by society, as well as economy. Within our economical system corporations consume these provided natural resources for producing goods or other services to create value for itself and society. As a

[33] Lawn, P. (2006), p.17.

consequence a throughput of resources through the company and its business-processes originates. By this process, and the consumption of goods and services natural resources are decimated and emissions, as well as wastes, are caused, ultimately absorbed by nature with its function as a sink. This absorption occurs by regulating functions provided by our ecological system, illustrated by the arrow from the "sink" to the "renewable source". The previously mentioned photosynthesis example is one instance of a regulating function absorbing emissions and produces new useful renewable resources out of it. In this concrete case it transfers carbon dioxide to oxygen. Further the figure contains a possible method used by economy to reduce environmental impact known as recycling. Finally corporations enable net psychic income being "something apart from money that you get from your job, and which gives you emotional satisfaction such as a feeling of being powerful or important."[34]

Figure 3 is pointing out that the business-view is especially interacting with nature by using its "provisioning" and "regulating" functions and in some way to the "supporting services" for getting site for their buildings or arable land for agrarian economy, which is not illustrated directly. But the "cultural and amenity" category is not compulsory connected to corporations in a direct way.

It follows that especially enterprises have, beside the usage of land, two noticeable interfaces to the ecosphere[35]:

- Input of resources and energy (using provisioning functions)
- Output of emissions, waste and products (using regulation functions)

---

[34] Financial Times Lexicon (2011), URL see references
[35] Cf. Seurig, S.A., Pick, E. (2001), p.157.

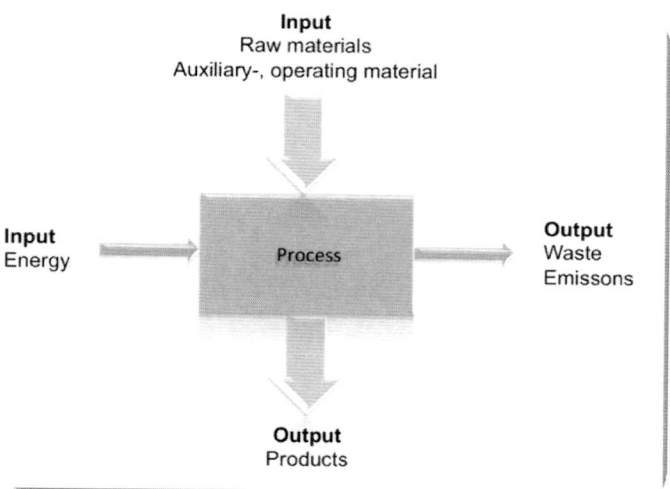

Figure 4 - Process Interfaces[36]

In Figure 4 input and output interfaces of corporations are separated into two different kinds of flows through the business-process of a corporation, as business-processes will be the focus for implementing a KEI framework. The first one is the primary material flow with its input of resources and output of products illustrated by the green arrows. The second one is the supporting flow with its input of energy and output of wastes and emissions illustrated by the red arrows. This separation into two different flows is necessary to divide the productive flow from the supporting flow and illustrates different kinds of interfaces from economy to nature.

---

[36] Seurig, S.A., Pick, E. (2001), p.157.

2.4 Health of nature

Based on these interfaces between economy and ecosphere it is possible to discuss the conditions of ecological health being necessary to set objectives for environmental protection.

Mentioning in advance that knowledge about ecosystem health and a general procedure of assessing diagnoses about it is still at the beginning and not as much developed as our knowledge about human health, for instance.[37] But as assessing ecological health is not primary to the practical part of this work it will be considered in a very superficial way. Nevertheless this information is helpful for corporations wanting to gather data about environmental health getting feedback about the effectiveness of their actions executed to reduce environmental impact, like optimizing a business-process based on its environmental impact. So when an ecological system is called and stated as healthy?

One assertion calls an ecological system healthy if it provides its inputs and functional services over indefinite time periods. This will only be the case if we are able to maintain it appropriately.[38] Another one states it as healthy whether it is able to provision goods and services to our society in a stable and sustainable way. Therefore it must have the ability to maintain its structure, as well as function, under external stress over time.[39] At last one is going to be introduced trying to explain environmental health from a sustainability point of view. If we want our world to be sustainable, it will be necessary to ensure that essential products and processes provided by our ecological system will be not used more quickly than they can be regenerated. Additionally only such an amount of waste should be discharged, that can be absorbed by nature.[40]

Hereby a certain similarity to the sustainable wood cutting notion is recognizable, as nature's products and processes should not be used more quickly than they can be regenerated. So in fact it is also saying not to live on the sub-

---

[37] Cf. Jorgensen, S.E. (2010), p.5.
[38] Cf. Milon, J.W., Shogren, J.F. (1995), p.28.
[39] Cf. Niccolucci, V., et al. (2010), p.425f.
[40] Cf. Wackernagel, M., Rees, W. (1996), p.7.

stances of nature, but on the revenues generated from it. It further enhances this statement by limited absorption processes that should not be exceeded.

These assertions have in common that goods and services provided by nature must be preserved for future generations, as they are basic needs of people, actually being the sustainable development thought of chapter 2.1. Thus health of environment is given if sustainable development is ensured. As a result health of environment is expressed by the ability of our ecological system to undo usage of its resources and impacts of its pollution caused by humanity. The relationship between ecology and sustainability could be identified as the sustainable availability of natures' provisioning and regulating functions. Strictly speaking, this understanding of natures' health is restricted. But there are other additional conditions necessary for assessing health of environment, like vital environment. Ecological health includes the availability of natures' supporting services, for instance, as a healthy environment needs space for development, so that a high diversity of animals and plants could exist.[41]

A further research specified health of our ecosystem in a more detailed way and identified the following aspects that are an expression of ecological health[42]:

- Homeostasis
- Absence of disease
- Diversity or complexity
- Stability or resilience
- Vigor or scope for growth
- Balance between system components

It contains the provisioning and regulating function within the aspects "homeostasis" or "stability or resilience" and expands the previously mentioned condition of ecological health.

As a matter of fact, it is neither exactly known when limitations of ecological functions are reached or even exceeded, nor the exact coherence of human- and economic activity to environmental damages making it really hard to set

---

[41] Cf. Schaltegger, S., Sturm, A. (1995), p.115f.
[42] Jorgensen, S.E., et al. (2010), p.11.

realistic and helpful usage and emission constraints, as well as objectives, for reducing environmental impact to corporations. Additionally, as mentioned in the introduction, developing countries also want economic prosperity, and cause more and more emissions and environmental damages. It follows that humanity must try to reduce their affects to our ecological system wherever possible and see the nature as an asset[43], or a capital[44] that is going to be invested in. However, there are some approaches to determine limitations to natures' functions by retaining the current amount of emissions and wastes connected with economic growth, which would imply to know the current impact to nature and increase eco-efficiency, so that more products or services can be produced with constant environmental impact.[45]

But how could corporations strategically reduce their environmental impact to contribute ensuring environmental health? To do so a method is needed to gather data about the actual impact of a single corporation on nature, as well as an approach to manage and direct it in a manner that is environmentally friendly and oriented to business strategy. Finally, it should provide information how to optimize or improve operational and organizational structure of businesses by ecological aspects. For that purpose the concept of Key Ecological Indicators will be introduced in the following chapter.

---

[43] Milon, J.W., Shogren, J.F. (1995), p.28. and Wackernagel, M., et al. (2006), p.246.
[44] Lawn, P. (2006), p.17.
[45] Cf. Faßenbender-Wynands, E., Seuring, S.A. (2001), p.151.

3. Key Ecological Indicators

In this chapter the concept of Key Ecological Indicators will be introduced. A common understanding of the term "Key Ecological Indicator" is necessary. Next some basic requirements to KEIs will be defined, as well as a classification of different kinds of KEIs. Then KEIs are considered from a macro-perspective for a better overview, and afterwards positioned within the micro-view. Finally, procedures to determine KEIs will be introduced and some indicators that might be KEIs, caused by its definition, will be presented.

3.1 What are KEIs?

To introduce the concept of KEIs a common understanding of the term Key Ecological Indicator is mandatory to avoid misunderstandings.
In current literature there is no definition for the term "Key Ecological Indicator". Thus it is not a common used expression, but there is a huge variety of different terminology in the context of ecology, like ecological indicator, ecological performance indicator, environmental accounting, environmental management system or eco-health assessment, which are partially synonyms.
First of all, one should ask what an indicator is in general. There is also a pretty obvious relation to Key Performance Indicators so it would be advisable to take a look at the definition of Key Performance Indicators as well. Finally, there are definitions for environmental indicators, which should also be considered.
At first it's necessary to know what the word indicator means. In chemistry, for instance, it is a tool to get information about the presence or absence of another chemical species usually induced by color.[46] In politics there are quantitative indicators, like gross domestic product to induce the economic situation and by comparison to the last years it displays the economic growth of a country.[47]

---

[46] Cf. Shakhaschiri, B.Z. (1989), p.39.

[47] Cf. Kesselmann, M., Krieger, J., (2009), p.13.

As a result of these two short examples it is a very universal term, and can be used for a very wide range of subjects. Moreover its purpose can be summarized as getting information about certain facts of interest.

Considering the business-context, indicators are also called performance measures or performance indicators, as they want to know how well the corporation performs. They are understood, similar to the politics example, as some kind of quantitative information about a company's internal or external situation.[48] These two terms evolve a certain issue concerning the distinction between indicators and measures. Frequently measures are stated as something that can be estimated directly, like water usage in liters for instance and indicators are quantitative assessments of variables that are estimated in an indirect way, for example job satisfaction.[49] Thus indicators can be built by one or several measures to reveal something that could not be measured directly. Therefore by speaking about indicators also measures could be meant. On the other hand, measures are a special subset of indicators. This understanding is illustrated in Figure 5.

Indicators should accomplish transparency by informing about operational facts in a very compact, relatively easy and concentrated manner.[50] This specification is necessary because businesses have the ability to gather a lot of data. There is so much data available that one is constantly overloaded with data and indicators are a possible way to limit complexity, as well as amount of information, to relevant and essential aspects.[51] This is usually done by aggregation and compression of much data into an indicator, but comes of course with loss of information and often leads to criticism about indicators in general.[52] Nevertheless they are indispensable to summarize data and take founded decisions within corporations, but this criticism should illustrate importance to take serious cogitations if defining and implementing indicators, as they are only a reflection of reality and could lead to wrong decisions if not appropriately defined and calculated. Moreover there are several kinds of indicators available. First there are

---

[48] Cf. Burkert, M. (2008), p.9.
[49] Cf. Bryman, A., Cramer, D. (2009), p.19.
[50] Cf. Hopfenbeck, et al. (1996), p.196.
[51] Cf. Gladen, W. (2008), p.11.
[52] Cf. Pape, J., et al. (2001), p.179.

present and past oriented measures of current internal business situations. Second there are normative indicators to set targets by specifying a quantitative number that should be reached and would be future oriented. Orientation indicators are used for comparison with external business situations, for instance the industry average and are also present oriented, but could give hints for setting new target indicators.[53]

From these shown understandings and kinds of indicators there could be derived two essential functions, namely a representation function and a management function.[54] Gladen mentioned another very relevant purpose of indicators, as they also possess a certain communication function by easing the communication process in an organization in terms of reports or discussions based on indicators.[55]

Thus functions of indicators are very wide spread, but the following three fundamental functions of indicators are identified:

- Representation function
    - Information function
    - Concentration function
- Communication function
- Management function

As a result, indicators have the purpose to represent the internal or external situation of organizations by quantitative information, concentrated by compression and ease the communication of its situation. If appropriately developed and calculated, they can help to take profound decisions and are a method to manage and lead organizations in a target-oriented manner by communicating target values in terms of indicators.

After the term "indicator" is adequately specified and different purposes were shown it comes to the differentiation of indicators and Key Performance Indica-

---

[53] Cf. Eichhorn, P. (1976), p.159f.
[54] Cf. Seidel, E., et al. (1998), p.10.
[55] Cf. Gladen, W. (2008), p.15.

tors. It is necessary to define KEIs. The word "key" commences an indicator that is very relevant and essential to the performance of an organization. It is stated as a "measure 'that matters' and ideally can be acted on."[56] The word "measure" should be renamed to the more general word "indicator", as KPIs could describe a relevant fact that couldn't be measured directly and would not follow the previous definition of "measure".

Like indicators in general, Key Performance Indicators also have a representation, communication and management function. The determination if an indicator is actually a KPI that is contained in this definition are the two words "that matters". To highlight and specify this aspect a definition from Parmenter will be introduced:

"KPIs represent a set of measures focusing on those aspects of organizational performance that are the most critical for the current and future success of an organization."[57]

In this definition the word "measure" is used instead of "indicator", but it says "a set of measures", which could actually measure something that couldn't be measured directly, for example the KPI "customer satisfaction". As it can't be meted directly it usually contains a set of measures that together hopefully indicate this fact of interest. Nonetheless it should also say a "set of indicators" instead of "measures" in terms of more flexibility, as KPIs could include several indirect facts of interest that are again induced by direct measures.

It follows that KPIs are identified as a special subset of indicators being strategically important for a corporation's performance and are current or future oriented, which implies that past measures cannot be and never were KPIs.[58] So their purpose is to "help an organization define and measure progress toward organizational goals."[59]

This temporal assumption causes another problem because the assertion that KPIs are current and future oriented is not specific enough. "Current oriented" can be understood differently for each individual organization, for example it

---

[56] Rasmussen, et al. (2009), p.23.
[57] Parmenter, D. (2010), p.4.
[58] Cf. Parmenter, D. (2010), p.7.
[59] Reh, F.J. (2011), URL see references

could mean all information of one day, month, quarter, year, or even since the foundation of the organization. It includes measures from the past, which does not agree with the statement saying KPIs are not past measures. Therefore the word "current" will be specified in the following. "Current" actually stands for a certain period of time of the past defined individually for each corporation depending on the understanding how the current business situation is represented. A corporation, for instance, that changed their business-process last year could understand "current" as an aggregation of information by one year, as it represents the actual state of the current business-process version. This statement contains the assumption that the word "current" means the time period since the last change of organizational or operational structure.

In the end KPIs are tied to strategic targets and could indicate the difference from present situation to predefined target situation.[60]

So they indicate a current situation in a particular manner and show how strong it differs from the targeted situation. To summarize the definition of KPIs, they

- indicate the performance of a particular, actual business situation,
- that is tied strategy
- by setting concrete target values, indicating difference between the strategically desired and the actual business situation.

After defining indicators and Key Performance Indicators it comes to the environmental reference. In literature there are attempts available to define the term "environmental indicator". One attempt is going to be introduced in the following. It describes an environmental indicator as "a mediate or immediate environmentally relevant quantity, formed as an absolute or relative number, which describes purposefully an operational situation with increased insight value."[61]

Thus environmental indicators have to express some kind of environmentally relevant information that show how much the environmental functions and services are used by corporations or illustrate the actual health status of our environment. For example an absolute environmental indicator is the total amount of

---

[60] Cf. Rasmussen, N., et al. (2009), p.23f.

[61] Kottmann, H., et al. (1999), p.7. (translated)

water used, or a relative one is the amount of water used per product, which are both part of the provisioning function of Mother Nature and fulfill the "environmentally relevant information" requirement. This specification further justifies the determination of health and function of nature, as they contained interfaces between ecology and economy, and thus contain references about what environmentally relevant information is.

Additionally the following statement concretizes this definition:

"Environmental indicators should reflect the objectives of environmental protection, which are set under consideration of sustainable economic activities".[62]

It results that environmental indicators should be derived from objectives of environmental protection and show the environmentally relevant information that is needed to optimize the corporation in a way that contributes to environmental protection.

With this understanding of indicators, Key Performance Indicators and environmental indicators, the question: "What are KEIs?" will be answered in the following. They are also understood as a certain subset of indicators the previous determined functions, like representation or management function of indicators apply in this case, too.

As stated out it is similar to the term "Key Performance Indicators", but the word "Performance" is substituted by "Ecological". So the performance of a corporation is not ultimately the primary aspect, but the ecological impact is the relevant information that is going to be quantified, implying KEIs being a subset of environmental indicators. Therefore a certain concretization is needed that enables to determine if an environmental indicator is actually a KEI. As an environmental indicator is derived from objectives from environmental protection this statement cannot be taken for identifying environmental indicators to be KEIs.

For this purpose the following statement considers the relation from KPIs to KEIs: "Key Ecological Indicators (…) are in fact special Key Performance Indicators"[63]. This is the reason why aspects and issues discussed for KPIs do also apply to KEIs, like the definition of the current business situation, which has to

---

[62] ebenda, p.4. (translated)
[63] Nowak, A., et al. (2010), p.3.

be considered if implementing KEIs. Moreover this statement enables to determine if an environmental indicator is actually a KEI based on the definition making an indicator a KPI.

As KPIs and KEIs are a special subset of indicators and additionally KEIs is a special subset of environmental indicators caused by their environmental reference. KPIs are understood as a strategic indicator that matters and is essential to the performance and success of a corporation. An indicator shows an internal or external business situation, which can be strategically relevant. It follows that KPIs are a certain subset of indicators. Because of identifying KEIs as special KPIs they are a subset of them.

As a result, linkage to strategy was the primary aspect that determined if an indicator is a KPI. This knowledge is used to specify whether an environmental indicator is a KEI. KEIs do not solely indicate a certain environmental fact but rather they should show environmental information, which are strategically relevant. As a result Key Ecological Indicators are understood as an

- indication of environmental impact concerning a particular, actual business situation,
- that is tied to strategy
- by setting concrete target values, inducing difference between the strategically desired and the actual business situation

To use this definition for visualizing KEIs in the practical part of this work it will be further specified in a more mathematical way:

KEIs are defined "as a tuple consisting of an Ecological Characteristics (EC) metric and a target value function based on the ecological goals one wants to achieve (defined by business strategy)."[64]

In conclusion an actual business situation is represented by ecological characteristics that express the usage of nature's goods and services by corporations identified in 2.3. Reference to strategy is ensured by a target value function that is derived from business strategy and can include the objective to ensure health of nature, discussed in 2.4. An example illustrates this definition: 'water con-

---

[64] Nowak, A., et al. (2011), p.6.

sumption of a corporation per year <= 100.000 liters'. It implicitly has the assumption that reducing water consumption is connected to a corporations' strategy.

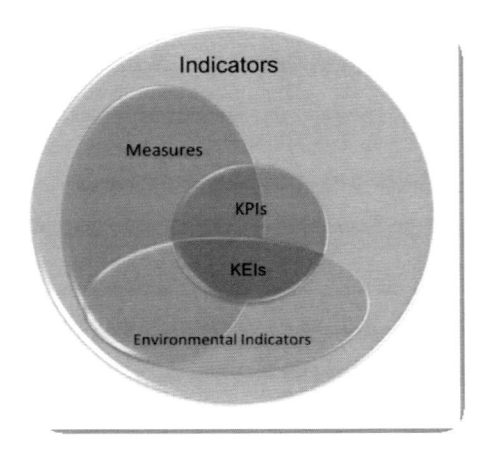

Figure 5 - Correlation of Indicators

Finally the assumed correlation of these different terms is illustrated in Figure 5. Depending on the responsibility toward ensuring sustainable development taken by a corporation, the set of KEIs would become larger if more responsibility is taken, as it would include more environmental indicators that are connected to strategy.

3.2 Requirements for KEIs

The previous definition set properties KEIs must fulfill. But there are further aspects needed for evaluating the quality of KEIs. In literature there are already plenty of requirements for classical indicators or indicator systems and some explicitly for environmental indicators available. Consequently requirements to indicators are also applicable to KEIs, as they are in fact a special subset of indicators. There are so many different requirements named in literature that a limitation to the most essential and relevant ones is necessary.

The first requirement that is going to be introduced is summarized under the term "economical requirement". It consists of the aspects time, quality, flexibility and profitability of information and consequently means that it should be worthwhile to take effort in gathering information and processing them to indicators. This is determined by setting the requirement that the gathering and processing procedure should cost less than, or at least be proportional to the benefits generated by it. Further this process should be executed within a certain period of time, so that these indicators are available at a point in time when they are usable and needed. Flexibility is mentioned in terms of a set of indicators and means that they should be adaptable. At last quality signifies an appropriate preparation of information for decision-making. These consisting aspects should be entirely optimized, as they are also related and have negative effects to each other.[65]

For example if the time attribute is optimized to a real-time collection of data and calculation of indicators, it will decrease profitability, as the needed infrastructure enabling real-time indicators is more expensive. Thus one has to consider whether real-time is really necessary to improve time and decrease profitability. Setting this general requirement actually covered a lot of different requirements that are named and listed by other authors, for example requirements like currency[66], availability[67] or acceptable costs[68]. Because of this generalization almost every set of requirements that have been found did include some kind of economical requirement. It illustrates that it is very relevant.

Measurability or quantification[69] is yet another frequently mentioned requirement. It means representing the fact of interest by a number. Achieving it is not easily feasible in each case, like measuring the mentioned customer satisfaction KPI. Nevertheless it is achieved by identifying a set of measures that might indicate it.

---

[65] Cf. Ösze, D. (2000), p.80.
[66] Cf. Kottmann, H., et al. (1999), p.19.
[67] Cf. Dietrich, E., et al. (2007), p.14.
[68] Cf. Jorgensen, S.E., et al. (2010), p.11.
[69] Cf. Pape, J., et al. (2001), p.184.

And there are further requirements like simplicity[70], verifiability[71], comparability[72] and reliability[73], which will not be explained as they mostly speak for themselves or are not that relevant to the requirements for KEIs.

However, there are some requirements particularly set for environmental indicators in literature. KEIs are a subset of environmental indicators and therefore requirements for environmental indicators can apply to them as well. Environmental indicators should:[74]

- address key issues
- be quantifiable
- be derived from process (modeling) data
- relate to other metrics commonly used in research and business decision-making processes

With key issues the big environmental problems could be meant, or issues within the corporation that exist concerning ecology, so environmental indicators should be connected to them. Quantification and measurability is also a requirement for ecological indicators. Derivation from process data offers the first evidence for a possible procedure to determine KEIs, discussed in section 3.5. The relation to other metrics is helpful for using these metrics for decision-making and is even necessary if aspects like eco-efficiency are going to be measured. This relation is not essential to KEIs so that it is not made a requirement for them.

With these several requirements for indicators and environmental indicators requirements for KEIs will be set for this work:

- Economical Requirement
- Relevancy (tied to strategy by target value)
- Measurability / Quantification

---

[70] Cf. Jorgensen, S.E., et al. (2010), p.11.
[71] Cf. Clausen, J. (1998), p.53.
[72] Cf. Kottmann, H., et al. (1999), p.19.
[73] Cf. Ösze, D. (2000), p.80.
[74] Harmsen, J., Powell, J.B. (2010), p.162.

- Environmental reference
- Transparency

The economical requirement does apply to KEIs with its contained aspects time, quality, flexibility and profitability. It is always a fundamental requirement in practice. Further it should fulfill the requirements "relevant" by connection to strategy and "environmental reference" by containing some kind of environmental impact. They result from the definition of KEIs. Moreover KEIs should also be measurable or quantifiable for decision-making and transparent to discuss how they are calculated or how well they express certain information.

3.3 Classification of KEIs

After setting requirements a classification is needed for a better structure and distinction of different kinds of KEIs. In advance there are many possibilities to classify them by the most varying aspects. Because of the fact that they are tied to strategy a wide range of different KEIs could possibly be identified.

A certain class was already mentioned, by thinking about health of environment. Depending on strategy, it results in KEIs for ecological quality, health or current ecological state. Another kind of KEIs expresses environmental stress caused by corporations and other entities using provisioning and regulating functions of nature. Moreover there are indicators for environmental management that enable to take decisions based on quantitative numbers. This classification is illustrated in Figure 6. It should be considered that environmental management indicators could contain both, environmental stress and environmental health indicators for managing environmental impact. As a result this separation is not distinct. Additionally indicators for environmental health are primary politically relevant and only huge corporations with a high environmental impact upon its region will gather such information to monitor and document the regional environmental status.[75] It can be used to indicate progress in protecting the regional environment and could show if taken environmental actions are effective.

---

[75] Cf. Kottmann, H., et al. (1999), p.9.

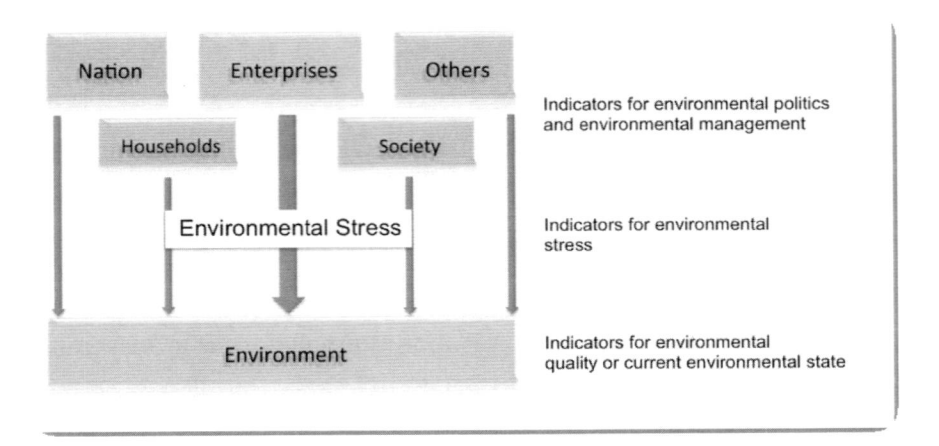

Figure 6 - Different Environmental indicators[76]

Another possibility is to classify KEIs based on their scale of unit. One unit is called "resource-based". That means for example the usage of water in liters or the weight of coal used. So it generally stands for the actual usage of resources or ejection of emission and wastes. Reconsidering the definition of KEIs, resource-based KEIs are an ecological characteristics metric consisting of one or more environmental impacts with the same scale of unit, like carbon dioxide emission or amount of all emissions in gram for example. These measured resource usages, emissions and wastes can also be transformed in a certain way to monetary values, so that costs of water or electricity are gathered. Advantages and disadvantages of this monetary evaluation are going to be discussed in section 3.5. The third level is artificial-based KEIs. To create a highly aggregated KEI, containing total environmental impact of a corporation in one ecological characteristics metric, different inputs and outputs with distinct scales of unit have to be aggregated. Thus artificial-based KEIs are calculated by a method that aggregates impacts to ecology that have different scales of unit.

Finally an approach based on the level of detail will be introduced. Measures, for example, "can be cascaded through an organization and tracked at different

---

[76] Clausen, J. (1998), p.55. (translated)

levels - such as the employee, process, plant, or product levels"[77]. Based on this insight KEIs are categorized by different abstraction levels within a corporation. This work differentiates three levels: products, processes and corporation level. In regard building a KEI Framework for business-processes, the process-level additionally contains the following subcategories: process, process-instance, activity and activity-instance and enables aggregation of KEIs for processes on different abstraction levels.

The classification in environmental management, environmental stress and environmental health indicators is actually not considered, as KEIs are some kind of environmental management indicators that again can consist of both environmental health and -stress indicators.

Corporation
(resource-, monetary-, artificial-based)

Processes
- Process
- Process-Instance
- Activity
- Activity-Instance

(resource-, monetary-, artificial-based)

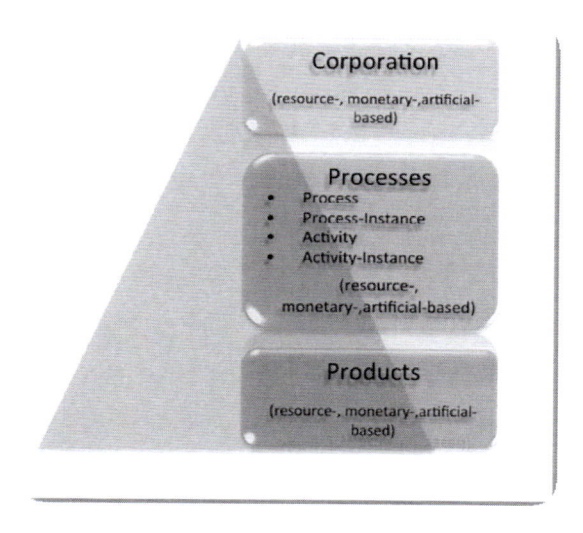

Products
(resource-, monetary-, artificial-based)

Figure 7 - Classification of KEIs[78]

In conclusion KEIs are categorized into corporation, processes and products, whereby the processes category is specified into process, process-instance, activity and activity-instance. In all categories they are distinguished by scale of

---

[77] Olson, E.G. (2009), p.27.
[78] Refers to: Kottmann, H., et al. (1999), p.11.

unit in resource-based, monetary-based and artificial-based KEIs, which is illustrated in Figure 7.

3.4 Positioning and usage of KEIs

To position KEIs two different perspectives upon environmental management will be outlined: the macro-view and the micro-view. As this work is concentrating on KEIs based on the business-context it primary relies on the micro-view of environmental management and will be the focus of this chapter. The consideration of the macro-view gives a better understanding of the correlation between macro- and micro-view and shows how big environmental problems outlined in the introduction of this work could ideally be solved.

3.4.1 Macro-view

In chapters one and two importance of environment to humanity has been shown and certain problems that currently exist have been outlined that society has to think about and in the end also has to find a solution. The issue is that corporations are not able managing and solving big environmental problems and ensure sustainable development themselves. Because one single enterprise has relatively little impact on ecology compared to the whole world. Additionally some corporations still have the classical hierarchy of systems in mind, introduced in section 2.2 on the left part of Figure 2. Thereby they see the environment as a completely public good and do not realize importance of ecology for their business to be sustainable, as well as for humanity to exist.

Thus ideally a higher authority would measure state of environmental health and set limits to humanity and economy for using resources, ejecting wastes and emissions. Further it would try to ensure health of nature, as well as gather and monitor current usages of resources, ejection of wastes and emissions of humanity. It results in some sort of KEIs on a macro basis, but instead of an actual business situation, the ecological situation is considered. The strategic target that these KEIs would be connected to is to ensure sustainable development including ensuring health of nature. Such an overall authority doesn't currently exist, as this would be a very hard and complex endeavor. It would involve all nations and governments to agree upon. So different other hierarchies within the macro-view can be identified[79]:

- Earth, Supranational region, National state and Region

The "Earth" level is the abovementioned absolute authority. Unfortunately this ideal authority is very unrealistic for managing environmental concerns in practice, as too much different nations and opinions do exist to implement such an endeavor.

The next level would be the "supranational region". This level is much more realistic, as a subset of all nations is trying to find solutions for environmental problems and discussing necessary limits and improvements to ensure sustainable development. This scenario has been actually done by the Kyoto-protocol, where different nations, like the European Union, United States, Japan, Russia and other nations, tried to discuss environmental problems and set limits and targets for emissions.[80] It "defines allowable greenhouse gas emissions for each industrialized country Party in terms of assigned amounts for the commitment period 2008-2012"[81]. But not all countries ratified the convention, thus did not commit to those defined targets. It follows that the "supranational region" solution is also very hard to realize to really ensure sustainable development and coordinate actions.

The "National State" level considers a single nation. Its government has the responsibility to ensure sustainable development by regulations. On this more specific level the problem with it is that total humanity has an impact on earth and not only a single nation. Individual efforts can be neutralized by other nations who did not realize importance of environmental health and sustainable development.

---

[79] Braun, B. (2002), p.142. (translated)
[80] Cf. Oberthür, S., Ott, H.E. (1999), p.13.
[81] Grubb, M., et al. (1999), p.115.

A "Region" is for example a federal state or an administrative district and would be a very local approach managing impact on environment on a macro-basis. As a result big environmental problems cannot be really solved on this level.

As different levels of the macro-view should manage the environmental impact, Key Ecological Indicators can be derived for each of them. These KEIs are not interested in the current business situation like the definition said, but in the current environmental status. For example some indicators exist for current health of environment within one region, but no general accepted indicators for all specific ecosystems are available.[82] Therefore this would be a very local, as well as hard and tedious endeavor, but first attempts like tradable or marketable emission permits[83] were introduced on the "supranational region" to manage the big environmental problems. They created market conformable structures so that corporations have to buy emission rights if they want to cause more emissions. If they emission less than permitted they could sell the right to cause emissions to other companies, so the issue progress in environmental protection could not be expressed in monetary value would be solvable on a macro-basis. As a result the macro-view is fundamental to actually solve big environmental problems that whole humanity and economy has and to set limits to use natures' functions, as well as to set extrinsic motivation and regulations for corporations.

The macro-view gives an insight in which context the micro-view takes place. This is helpful for a better understanding of the correlation between macro- and micro-view.

3.4.2 Micro-view

Like the macro-view, the micro-view is also trying to reduce impact on ecosphere and may contribute to solve big environmental problems, but the considered environmental impact is limited on a single enterprise. This contribution is caused by intrinsic and extrinsic motivations mentioned before. To operationalize this endeavor for corporations a concept called environmental manage-

---

[82] Cf. Jorgensen, S.E. (2010), p.5.
[83] Cf. Lesourd, J.B., Schilizzi, S.G.M. (2001), p.27.

ment (EM) evolved. For EM a very general specification is "management of environmental aspects of a company"[84]. So everything that a corporation does concerning environment is stated as some kind of environmental management. It means that it is a cross-departmental function[85]. This understanding will be further concretized, as it is only helpful to state KEIs being some kind of environmental management. Nevertheless by analyzing what an EM is and consists of this analysis could contain hints for building a KEI framework.

At first the ambition of EM will be considered. Its purpose is to plan, control, monitor and improve all actions concerning environmental protection within an enterprise, as well as to lead the company and employees in an environmental-oriented manner.[86]

Actually KEIs follow a similar ambition. They include to plan (identifying strategy including environmental aspects and set target values), monitor (getting environmental impact of the actual business situation expressed by a calculated ecological characteristics metric), control (visualizing KEIs indicating difference between actual and strategically desired situation) and improve (identifying and executing actions realizing strategy) a corporation regarding its environmental impact that is connected to strategy.

---

[84] Harmser, J., Powell, J.B. (2010), p.220.

[85] Cf. Schaltegger, S., Sturm, A. (1995), p.23.

[86] Cf. Kamiske, G.F., et al. (1995), p.4.

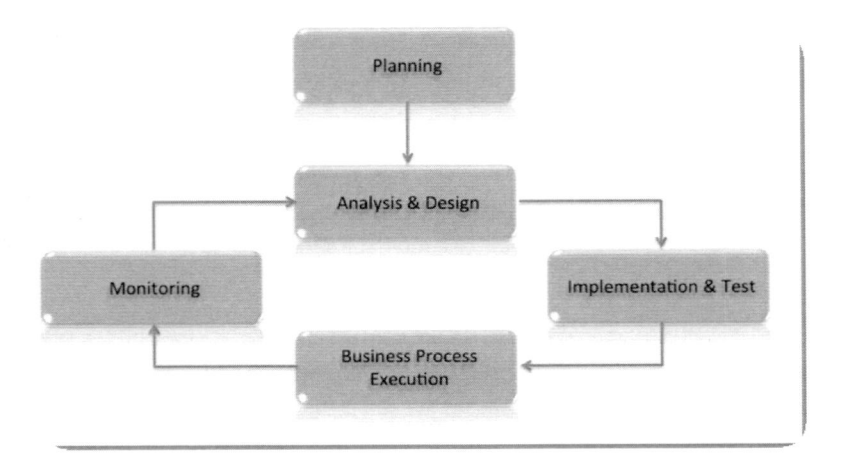

Figure 8 - BPM Lifecycle[87]

A similarity is recognizable between the ambition of an EM and the business process management (BPM) lifecycle illustrated in Figure 8. Both management approaches plan, monitor, control and improve certain aspects of a corporation, whereby the function "control" is contained within step "analysis & design" of the BPM lifecycle and the function "improve" is implicitly contained by the lifecycle itself. But the BPM lifecycle is not focusing on decreasing environmental impact of a corporation, but on improvement of business-process and thus contains the phase "implementation & test" and "business process execution".

So in regard identifying how to calculate KEIs connected to strategy for optimizing business-processes by the BPM lifecycle, it will be evaluated how environmental relevant information is gathered within EM. This procedure can be adopted to gather environmental data about business-processes. Therefore the concept of EM must be made concrete in a certain way. This is done by an environmental management system (EMS).

For a further consideration of an EMS, a statement will be introduced:

"An environmental management system (…) is the part of businesses' overall management system that includes organizational structure, planning activities, responsibilities, practices, procedures, processes, and resources for develop-

---

[87] Refers to: Kress, M. (2010), p.25.

ing, implementing, achieving, reviewing, and maintaining an environmental policy."[88]

An environmental policy "is a set of principles and intentions used to guide decision making about human management of environmental capital and environmental services."[89] Consequently it is connected to certain environmental objectives and determines what should be done within a corporation concerning environmental impact.

Following these two statements, KEIs are also part of an environmental management system and overall management system caused by their definition to be special environmental indicators that are strategically relevant.

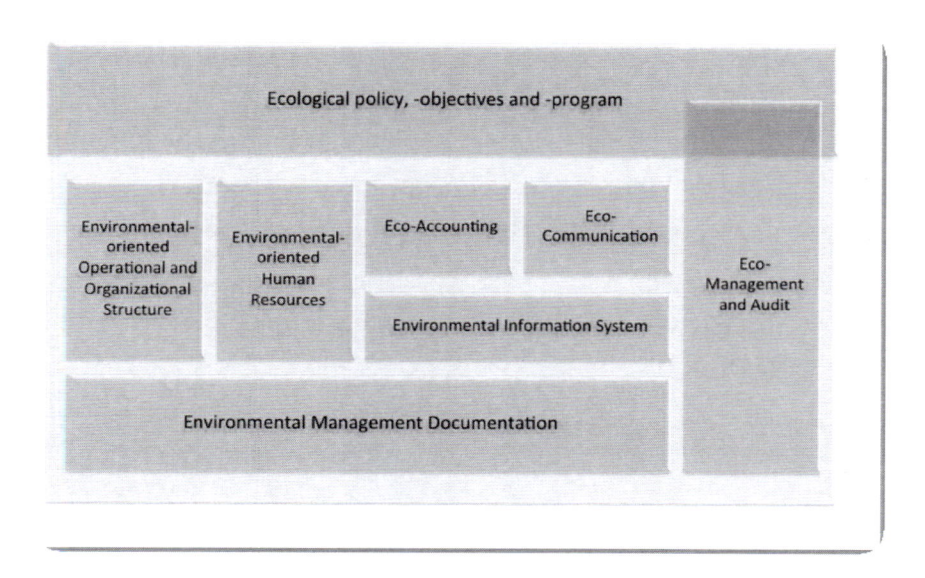

Figure 9 - Components of an EMS[90]

As one can see in Figure 9 an environmental management system includes a lot of different aspects and components that have to be considered and implemented. In regard to the practical part of this work these components will be evaluated to identify whether they are applicable for building a KEI Framework for business-processes.

---

[88] Friedman, F.B. (2003), p.68.
[89] Roberts, J. (2011), p.2.
[90] Große, H., et al. (2000), p.33. (translated)

The component eco-policy has been illustrated already, which is in case of KEIs the business strategy including environmental goals.

Next the component "eco-accounting" is considered. The purpose of accounting could be summarized as support of management in all decision-making processes.[91]

In terms of eco-accounting it supports management in making decisions based on environmental objectives and accomplishes them. It means that all planning, controlling, monitoring and decision-making activities should be related and aligned to concrete environmental objectives.[92] It signifies, besides economical aspects, to consider especially aspects of the environment when decisions will be made. To operationalize this goal eco-accounting contains functions like analysis of environmental performance and weak points, planning, controlling, monitoring of environmental performance, suggestions for improvements and improvement of information quality for internal plus external communication.[93]

It consequently reveals that eco-accounting is a very central component of an EMS. As a result it is usable for identifying how to get environmental relevant information for optimizing processes by the BPM lifecycle. Thus it is relevant for building a KEI framework and justifies analyzing it in detail.

---

[91] Cf. Schaltegger, S., Sturm, A. (1995), p.15.

[92] Cf. Faßenbender-Wynands, E., Seuring, S.A. (2001), p.141.

[93] Cf. Schaltegger, S., Sturm, A. (1995), p.15.

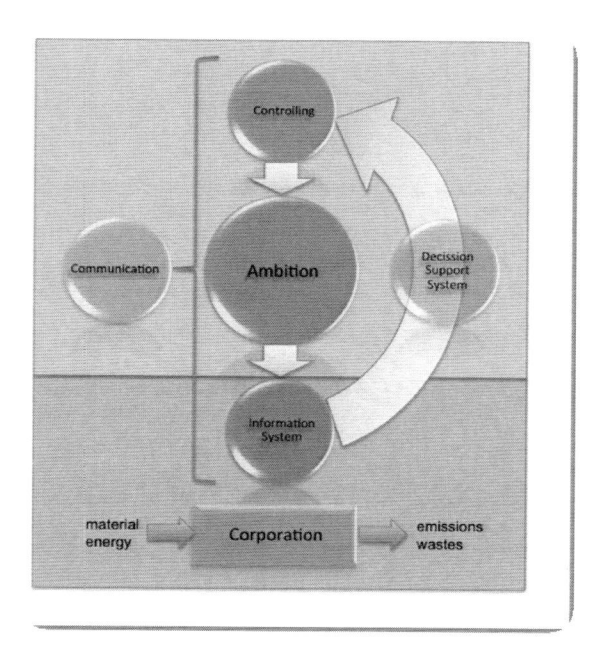

Figure 10 - Modules of Eco Accounting[94]

Figure 10 contains modules that are needed for environmental-accounting and their correlation to each other. The module "ambition" was mentioned by the environmental policy of an EMS. It determines the focus of eco-accounting by formulating ecological and economical goals that are differentiated in general objectives of corporations (defined by top-management), and specific ones (defined during the eco-accounting process), like annual objectives, departmental objectives or detailed objectives. The person being responsible for the corresponding subject defines these specific objectives.[95] An example for such a person is the process-owner being responsible for a specific business-process and sets specific objectives to the process he owns.

The foundation of an eco-accounting system is an "information system". Its purpose is gathering environmental data being strategically relevant, as well as identifying substances and energies used by a corporation.[96] Moreover it in-

---

[94] Refers to: Schaltegger, S., Sturm, A. (1995), p.21.
[95] Cf. Schaltegger, S., Sturm, A. (1995), p.21.
[96] Cf. ebenda, p.22.

cludes measuring these substances and energies, and further environmental costs that are by them expressed in monetary values with regard to the specific situation of a corporation.[97]

Finally, gathering environmental data is pursuing the goal to evaluate data from existing systems, as production planning and scheduling, accounting or material management, to reduce amount of data that has to be gathered.[98]

Unfortunately raw data are not usable making management decisions, showing necessity establishing another module called "decision support system". It aggregates and/or processes this raw data to calculate environmental indicators, present this information to the relevant authority, and enables identifying demand for actions.[99]

After decisions have been made it is requisite to ensure its execution and controlling its success. Reasons and extends of discrepancies to objectives have to be analyzed. Hereafter follows identification of new objectives or actions.[100] Resulting in the lifecycle illustrated in Figure 10.

Last there is the module "communication". Eco-Accounting provides the basis to internally and externally communicate ones achievements in following environmental objectives.[101]

Reconsidering the components of an EMS, eco-accounting is correlated to eco-policy, -objectives and -programs by the module "ambition". It does have to contain an environmental information system to get data about the usage of provisioning-, regulating- and supporting services- functions provided by nature. These data are processed and aggregated to environmental indicators by the module "decision support system". On this basis actions are executed and controlled by the module "controlling", enabling an environmental-oriented operational and -organizational structure, as well as eco-management. As Figure 9 does not contain the components "decision support system" and "controlling", it is assumed that hey are included to the eco-accounting component. Moreover environmental-accounting provides information for eco-communication.

---

[97] Cf. ebenda, p.25.
[98] Cf. ebenda, p.27.
[99] Cf. ebenda, p.22.
[100] Cf. Schaltegger, S., Sturm, A. (1995), p.22.
[101] Cf. ebenda, p.22.

As a result eco-accounting actually covers or is the basis for most EMS components. Some of them were not mentioned, for example environmental-oriented human resources. It contains that employees will be selected based on their awareness about environmental problems and do contribute to reduce environmental impact of the corporation by their personal interest. It is relevant because "the culture of individual organizations, sites or even departments can affect how a system is used"[102] and people that work in a corporation determine its culture. Resulting in an example why an environmental-oriented human resources department is absolutely necessary and important for an EMS. Additionally all these different modules should be documented in a certain way, which is necessary for evaluating the quality of the EMS internally and externally. The external evaluation of environmental management is necessary for existing standards like ISO 14000[103] or EMAS[104]. Both of them can be certified by an auditing process, which will analyze those different components and approve or refuse its accordance to those standards and therefore need some sort of documentation.

"The outputs of an EMS will reflect values of the organization (…) [and] may have an effect on culture, but this will be an evolutionary and controlled process."[105] Stating that the scope or actual implementation of an EMS depends on the corporates' values that are indicated by its understanding of hierarchy of economy, ecology and society, and the responsibility taken to ensure sustainable development (see chapter 2).

In terms of building a KEI framework for business-processes, without already having an existing environmental management system that gathers environmental information, especially the modules needed for environmental-accounting have to be considered. Justified by the fact that KEIs are special kinds of environmental indicators and environmental-accounting with its modules does provide the functionality to calculate environmental indicators.

---

[102] Sheldor, C., Yoxon, M. (2002), p.5.

[103] ISO 14000 (2011), URL see references
[104] EMAS (2011), URL see references
[105] Sheldor, C., Yoxon, M. (2002), p.7.

Reconsidering the purpose of this work illustrated in Figure 1, all modules of environmental-accounting have to be implemented to execute all steps. But as the purpose of this work is limited to the first three steps the KEI framework has to include the modules "ambition" for defining KEIs, "information system" by establishing a measurement system, and "decision support system" by deploying a management dashboard that can indicate demand for actions for optimization. Thus modules "controlling" and "communication" are not considered.

As this work focuses on KEIs for business-processes the box "corporation" illustrated in Figure 10 that says an information system gathers data about the overall company, is changed to processes. It consequently reveals connection between the BPM lifecycle and environmental-accounting, as it is focusing on corporation level and thus has to gather data about the execution of processes and its environmental impacts.

The micro-view consequently shows how environmental data can be measured and enabled getting knowledge about modules needed for calculating KEIs.

Afterward it is necessary to identify how KEIs can be used within the microview. As they are defined as special environmental indicators the usages of environmental indicators do also apply to KEIs. With this information the following usage examples of KEIs are identified:[106]

- Illustration of environmental changes within time
- Detection of optimizing potentials
- Feedback for motivating employees
- Foundation for communication (reports and explanations concerning the environment)
- Evaluation of environmental performance
- Decision-support for environmental investments
- Early warning system for corporate deficiencies
- Determination and monitoring of environmental objectives
- Identification of market opportunities and potentials in reducing costs
- Support for auditing-process (certification)

---

[106] Pape, J., et al. (2001), p.179. (translated)

Additionally they are used in a further way:

- Ensure environmental actions to be tied to strategy

3.5 Determination of KEIs

With this chapter it will be shown how step one of Figure 1 is executed. As the definition specifies, KEIs indicate a particular, actual business situation with its environmental impact by an ecological characteristics metric. Its connection to strategy is ensured by a target value function. Unfortunately the connection to strategy makes it hard to find general accepted KEIs for corporations that do apply to all industries and companies because their strategies, designated objectives and targets about reducing environmental impacts are often diverse. Thus this section is rather trying to illustrate different methods how KEIs can be identified, than defining concrete KEIs. Nevertheless some environmental indicators will be presented that might be KEIs, depending whether they are strategically relevant to a corporation.

The definition of KEIs actually enables two possible approaches or procedures to determine KEIs:

The first one would begin with the definition of a strategy containing environmental aspects. Afterwards it is operationalized by objectives and goals that should be followed or reached, called the overall objectives in environmental-accounting. It is the execution of the "ambition" module of environmental-accounting. Whereby these overall objectives could also contain different sub-objectives to specify and determine how exactly these overall objectives are fulfilled. Moreover specific objectives are set to define a status in which the overall objective is met, resulting in the identification of KEIs. Next the current business situation with its environmental impact is determined and measured in regard to aggregate and/or process this data to get the defined KEIs. This enables the possibility to reveal the difference between the strategically desired and the actual business situation. Depending on the specific objective that was set, gathering the actual target value for a KEI is enabled. For example, if one specific objective is to reduce electricity consumption by twenty percent the concrete amount of electricity to be reduced is settable after measuring the KEI. This procedure will be stated as a top-down[107] determination of Key Ecological Indicators. Actually it is the reason why the requirement "derivation from process (modeling) data" identified for environmental indicators was actually not made a requirement to KEIs because this wouldn't be a top-down approach.

Another possibility is to monitor a corporation by the "information system" module of environmental-accounting. It would analyze interfaces a corporation has to the environment by determining substances and energies used. Next these are measured and calculated and/or aggregated to ecological characteristic metrics. With this information the specific objectives can be set with concrete target values. Afterwards it will be determined whether they match to overall objectives that express the strategy. The issue resulting with this approach is that it possibly results in environmental indicators and not KEIs because they could miss the strategic reference. This approach is stated as a bottom-up determination[108] of Key Ecological Indicators.

Both approaches are illustrated in Figure 11. Furthermore the vision is added and influences or determines strategy. Additionally the illustration contains information about the scope considered to identify environmental impact and is the reason why "corporation n" is illustrated in the background, connected by an information flow arrow to "corporation".

The mentioned approaches actually are the result of the lifecycle that environmental-accounting does have. The top-down determination is used if KEIs are identified the very first time without having an existing environmental-accounting system. After it is implemented and KEIs are measured it results in a bottom-up determination. It enables to set target values for specific objectives or even could identify new aspects that were not considered. So it may enable to identify a new strategy. Over time it results in a sequence of top-down and bottom-up derivations, whereby the modules "ambition" and "information system" are not newly created but altered or expanded. To prove this mutual dependency, a

---

[107] Cf. Gladen, W. (2008), p.233.
[108] Cf. ebenda, p.233.

work from Simons will be presented. He tried to show the relation between vision, strategy, target values and actions. The vision or mission of a company determines its business strategy. Moreover performance measures and target values are derived from this strategy, leading to certain actions contributing to implement it. He identified that performance measures and target values as well as executed actions have an impact on the business strategy itself.[109] Thus the outlined mutual dependency between top-down and bottom-up derivation is supported by this knowledge.

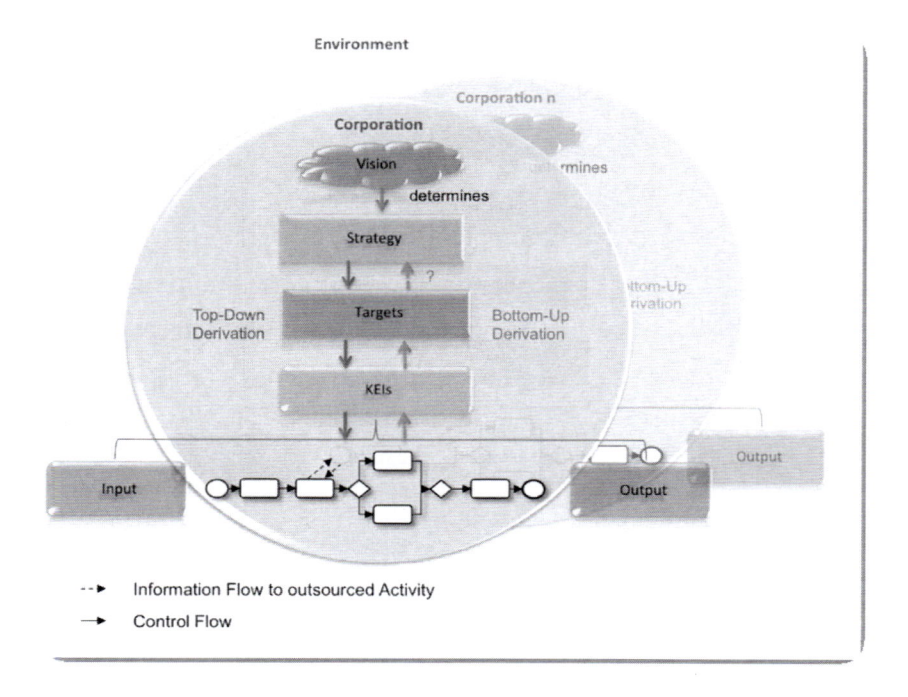

Figure 11 - Derivation of KEIs

Thus one has to think about two fundamental aspects for determining KEIs namely defining a strategy including overall objectives, derive specific objectives out of it (ambition), and measure the actual or current environmental impact to calculate KEIs that are tied to this ambition (information system and decision support system).

---

[109] Cf. Gladen, W. (2008), p.47.

As the identified requirements made to KEIs demanded a concrete correlation to nature, it is obligatory to analyze and identify the concrete impact from corporations to nature. Section 2.3 already illustrated the relationship of corporations to ecology and which functions of nature are primary used. Thus a step to build a basis for determining Key Ecological Indicators, if not already available, would be to acquire information about the input and output of the economic activities that is connected to nature and thereby fulfills this requirement. This foundation can be build by substance- and energy flux analysis, containing subjects like used materials or resources and energy consumption or ejected wastes and emissions to air and water.[110] The more aspects and details are covered by this analysis the better the real impact on nature can be shown, but because of high complexity the covered aspects usually have to be limited.[111] If the completeness requirement should be fulfilled, which is often a requirement to indicator-systems, all impacts have to be considered and the law of conservation of mass and energy must be complied. As a result, it is possible to determine energies and substances in a full or light approach.[112] The full determination is more complex and could possibly decrease the economical requirement made to KEIs, which is actually one reason why the completeness requirement was not set. Disregarding some aspects is permitted, because not all aspects posses the same relevance for ecology, as well as a corporations' strategy. This disregard and the resulting uncertainty should be known or documented in some way to ensure transparency and comparability of results.[113]

As a matter of fact the specific business situation has to be considered too by this analysis. Various corporations use and eject different energies and substances so it is hard to identify all possible substance and energies. Nevertheless there are several universal classes that can be identified for determining these flows and then be specified for an individual case. Harmsen and Powell

---

[110] Cf. Seurig, S.A., Pick, E. (2001), p.154.
[111] Cf. Müller, A. (2010), p.128.
[112] Cf. Schaltegger, S., Sturm, A. (1995), p.26.
[113] Cf. Seurig, S.A., Pick, E. (2001), p.156.

identified the following basic categories to express the inputs and outputs that corporations could have concerning nature:[114]

- Energy
- Material Intensity
- Water
- Land
- Emissions
    - Atmospheric (Acidification, Global warming, Human health, Ozone depletion, Photochemical ozone)
    - Aquatic (Acidification, Oxygen demand, Eco toxicity, Eutrophication)
    - Land (Toxic waste disposal, Nontoxic waste disposal)

These categories should be more specified, through identifying substances and energies within them that are actually used or ejected by a corporation. For example the category "atmospheric emissions" could contain gases that are the cause for global warming as carbon dioxide, nitrous oxide or methane[115], which should be persisted by the "information system" component if a corporation does eject them. So the result of energy and substance flux analysis is the substances and energies a corporation does actually use and emit.

Another question that rises for substance and energy flux analysis is the scope of environmental impact. It should include different emission scopes, which have to be considered:[116]

- Directly produced emissions
- Indirect emissions from purchased stuff
- Indirect emissions from outsourced activities

Considering directly produced emissions in this analysis is taken for granted and doesn't need further explication. Indirect emissions from outsourced activi-

---

[114] Harmser, J., Powell, J.B. (2010), p.10.
[115] Cf. Windsor, S. (2010), p.15f.
[116] Olson, E G. (2009), p.93.

ties and purchased stuff are not that obvious to regard. They must be gathered, which is why Figure 11 contained information flow to other companies. If indirect emissions would not be considered a corporation could reduce its environmental impact by simply outsourcing activities or buying stuff. In this way the real environmental impact will be not reduced, as the outsourced activities still have an environmental impact. Thus indirect emissions should be considered to set the correct motivation for reducing emissions. It enables that partners and purchased goods and services can be selected based on the emissions they cause and a corporation could not become environmentally friendly by outsourcing activities that harm the ecosphere the most. Moreover it should also consider used resources from purchased stuff and outsourced activities. This defined scope results in the ability to optimize environmental impact of companies and business-processes by changing and managing external partners or suppliers.

After energy and substance flux analysis is executed, the next step for calculating KEIs is to identify which energies and substances will be meted that are relevant for strategy. After these substances and energies are measured this data has the potential to be KEIs and can be aggregated or used to calculate further relative or absolute indicators or transform it to monetary- or artificial-based ones. The identified and meted energies and substances are the building set for creating further environmental indicators and KEIs, which illustrates the high flexibility of a full-determination and measurement of energies and substances for calculating KEIs.

In literature there are plenty examples for environmental indicators available that can be build on the basis of measured energies and substances.

Because there are so many different environmental-indicators, just some chosen examples will be shown in the following to give a little perception of different environmental indicators that depending on the corporates' strategy might be KEIs.

Müller specified relative environmental indicators, like recycling rate, which is calculated by identifying two resource-based indicators named amount of recycled material per anno and total material usage per anno. These two absolute measures are set in relation to each other to calculate the recycling rate, which would assume that the current business situation is expressed by one year. He identified more relative indicators for the categories material, energy, waste and emissions[117]. Other authors identified environmental indicators for financial[118], industry[119] or trading[120] companies. Thereby indicators like the amount of water used per process, percentage of a specific resource compared to whole resource usage of one process-instance or percentage of a specific kind of transportation were identified.

These introduced examples were mostly KEIs for environmental stress whose scale of unit is resource-based. Yet resource-based KEIs have a certain disadvantage caused by the fact of various scale of units, like electricity consumption could be gathered in kW/h and used material would be expressed in kg. This difference makes it very hard to aggregate measured inputs and outputs into KEIs that expresses total environmental impact, for instance. To solve this problem there are approaches to transform these environmental impacts to monetary values. It is an easy ongoing if a market prices does exist, for example the costs for one kilogram of wood. If such a market price is not available some other approaches established to evaluate costs of resource-based indicators, for example multiplying it by a shadow price called the damage cost approach or by multiplying it with maintenance costs that arise to undo the environmental impact[121] like for example the costs for planting such an amount of trees that would undo the emission of carbon dioxide caused by a company. Moreover the macro-view plays a certain role for this monetary transformation, as it could create a market for different environmental impacts, like the mentioned tradable or marketable emission permits.

A significant problem with this will be the transformation, as it is not always possible to determine a value expressed in money. This could be the case if there is no market, which would determine a price to the ejection or usage of re-

---

[117] Cf. Müller, A. (2010), p.134f.
[118] See Seicel, E. et al. (1998a), p.175ff.
[119] See Seicel, E. et al. (1998b), p.141ff.
[120] See Feller, M. et al. (1998), p.215ff.
[121] Cf. Dietz S., Neumayer, E. (2006), p.129.

sources.[122] Moreover even if a market price would exist or created on a macro-basis this would not ultimately be a real expressed impact to the environment. A manager claimed that one could not say a square meter of rainforest is worth 600$, because if they are vanished they will not renew themselves and therefore can't be monetarily valued.[123] Thus monetary KEIs would not express a realistic environmental impact, but would simply provide an intrinsic motivation for enterprises that didn't realize their social responsibility to reduce the usage and emission of resources. Additionally they help to limit amount of information by aggregation, but of course lose information to really identify demand for action to reduce environmental impact.

The last group is artificial-based KEIs, as eco-efficiency. Eco-efficiency could be calculated as a relative indicator that relates environmental impact to the unit of output or a monetary unit. Two possibilities exist to increase eco-efficiency. First increase unit of output or monetary unit with consistent environmental impact and second reduce environmental impact with consistent unit of output or monetary unit.[124] As a consequence it is an indicator calculated by monetary- and resources-based KEIs. Another example for artificial-based KEIs is the ecological footprint. It is an approach developed by Wackernagel and Rees[125] that tries to express the whole environmental impact by the amount of land in square meters needed to anticipate the usage of goods and services provided by nature.[126] So actually for every substance or energy that is used or ejected some kind of transformation is needed, which will determine how much land would be needed to undo its impact. Such an approach is stated as valuation methods[127]. Every substance gets a factor or weighting appended that would express the environmental damage compared to other substances. Its ambition is to aggregate different kinds of substances and energies with distinct scales of units to a highly aggregated indicator. The issue was already briefly mentioned, because such an evaluation of loading is always subjective and would not illustrate a real

---

[122] Cf. Lintott, J. (2006), p.86.
[123] Cf. Buß, E. (2007), p.213f.
[124] Cf. Faßenbender-Wynands, E., Seuring, S.A. (2001), p.151.
[125] See Wackernagel, M., Rees, W. (1996)
[126] Cf. ebenda, p.3.
[127] Cf. Schaltegger, S., Sturm, A. (1995), p.36.

environmental impact.[128] This is why some authors outline that highly aggregated indicators cannot be calculated, as their measure is too diverse.[129]

After presenting some environmental indicators and discussing some advantages and disadvantages as well, one should ask how many KEIs should be selected to manage environmental impact based on strategy. As they should reduce information to relevant aspects, it is pretty obvious that not an endless amount of KEIs can be picked. Therefore the amount should be constraint to more or less seven KEIs for one person that tries to manage a certain aspect like a single business-process.[130]

Finally some basic principles[131] will be introduced that are used to ensure ecological sustainability, which is part of sustainable development and could help corporations to identify a strategy including environmental concerns or in terms of environmental-accounting the ambition:

1. Regeneration (renewable resources should not be used faster than they can regenerate)
2. Substitution (non-renewable resources should be replaced by renewable ones if possible)
3. Adaption (emission of substances and energy should not be greater then nature can handle)

This leads to three different goals that a corporation could follow by strategy to protect the environment: Resource-, emission- and risk objectives. Raw resources should be preserved or saved, emissions and wastes prevented, reduced, reused or disposed, and risks reduced, avoided or restricted.[132] With these objectives a contribution to sustainable development can be made by corporations and is helpful to identify a strategy concerning the environment. Moreover several hints were conducted by mentioning intrinsic and extrinsic motivations for corporations investing effort in reducing environmental impact.

---

[128] Cf. ebenda, p.36f.
[129] Cf. Pape, J., et al. (2001), p.184.
[130] Cf. Gladen, W. (2008), p.14.
[131] Kanning, H., Müller, M. (2001), p.18. (translated)
[132] Cf. Müller, A. (2010), p.27.

4. Building a KEI Framework for Business-Processes

In the following the practical part of this work will be done. It includes the achievement of steps one, two and three shown in Figure 1. Section 3.4.2 identified that KEIs are part of an environmental management system. Within an EMS they are primarily assigned to environmental-accounting with its required modules. A subset of modules needed for environmental-accounting is selected to get environmental relevant information. For the purpose of this work the modules "ambition", "information system" and "decision support system" are needed. These are contained in Figure 10. They will be implemented to gather environmental data about process execution. It enables to use the BPM lifecycle to optimize processes in terms of decreasing environmental impact based on strategy.

Actually the ambition is not completely part of the technical implementation of the KEI Framework, as it is assuming that strategy, overall- and specific objectives are pre-defined. But they are expressed implicitly by corresponding target values that are persisted by the framework. To identify KEIs a strategy is needed that determines which environmental data will be measured. Interfaces of business-processes to nature must be identified by energy and substance flux analysis in a full or light determination approach.

By measuring these substances and energies, KEIs are going to be calculated and visualized on a management dashboard, which is the "decision support system" module. It is necessary for the "analysis" phase of the BPM lifecycle. The other modules "controlling" and "communication" of environmental-accounting are not explicitly considered for this KEI framework, but are enabled by providing information that both modules need.

The context of the underlying case study will be introduced to show how KEIs can be identified and visualized. Afterwards the concrete architecture of this KEI framework for business-processes will be explained in detail and several design choices that have been considered are going to be discussed.

4.1 Introducing the Case study

ESOR Inc. (Environmentally Sustainable Online Reseller) and its ordering business-process (see Figure 12) is the fictive company used for this case study. It is an online reseller company that offers different products exclusively through its online-shop in the business-to-consumer (b-to-c) and business-to-business (b-to-b) segment. It is hard for ESOR to ensure uniqueness and competitiveness as the amount of competitors is very high in this market. Therefore management thinks about a new strategy that could lead to a competitive advantage and differentiate ESOR from their rivals. After they thought about several opportunities they came to the conclusion that supplementing their existing strategy by environmental aspects would offer a good opportunity to ensure lasting competitiveness and improve their reputation. Further they identified that their customers are getting more eco-sensible and some customers in the b-to-b segment want information about the environmental impact that is caused by ordering their products from ESOR for their own environmental management system. Finally they detected a high risk of new regulations for environmental protection that could be minimized by including environmental aspects to their objectives and anticipate new regulations. They follow the stakeholder concept and realized that many of their stakeholders see environmental protection and sustainable development as very essential. The shareholders also realized an economic potential in reducing environmental impact. Therefore a sustainability strategy would be a good and promising opportunity. So there are intrinsic as well as extrinsic motivations for ESOR to see environmental protection as strategically relevant. To implement and manage this sustainability strategy they want to build a basis for an environmental management system by deciding to adopt the concept of KEIs for optimizing business-processes connected to their sustainability strategy. This will be realized prototypically for one business-process by implementing eco-accounting modules that enable to execute the BPM lifecycle in terms of environmental impact. This makes it possible to identify opportunities for optimization and the need for action in the business-process. It is planed to expand this endeavor to all business-processes and get environmental information for all of them.

As the ordering process is one of most frequently executed processes it has a high potential to reduce environmental impact. So it is the first one that is going to be expanded with environmental information. Figure 12 illustrates the existing ordering process in Business Process Modeling Notation (BPMN). This will be described in the following and is needed to identify the processes' interfaces by substance- and energy flux analysis later on. It ensures the "environmental reference" requirement made to KEIs:

The customers place an order through the online shop, which will send a message containing all items ordered and the address information. This starts the ordering process of ESOR. First it checks whether these products are in stock in an adequate quantity in their warehouse. If this is not the case the products will be ordered from their suppliers. There are only two different suppliers. If supplier one has not all needed products in stock they will be ordered from supplier two. So there is no further logic for the selection of suppliers implemented. After all ordered products are in stock in their warehouse a shipment service of another company will be notified to ship the delivery to the customer. The customer will be informed about the shipment of his order. At the same time the bank will be notified about the payment method and will inform ESOR whether the money transfer from the customer to their account is completed. The business process is completed successfully after shipment and payment activities have been executed. The described process is simplified to essential aspects and only describes the relevant information for this work, like the activities "order items", "shipment" and "payment" contains some more steps, which are skipped for better intelligibility. For example, it is not visualized if the ordered items are neither available in the warehouse, nor from the suppliers the customer will be informed about the cancelation of his order. Further it is not shown that the payment process contains the activities "request authorization", "get credit card details" and "notify customer paid". Different exceptions that could occur are also not visualized. And like in practice the exact business-processes of the partners are not known.

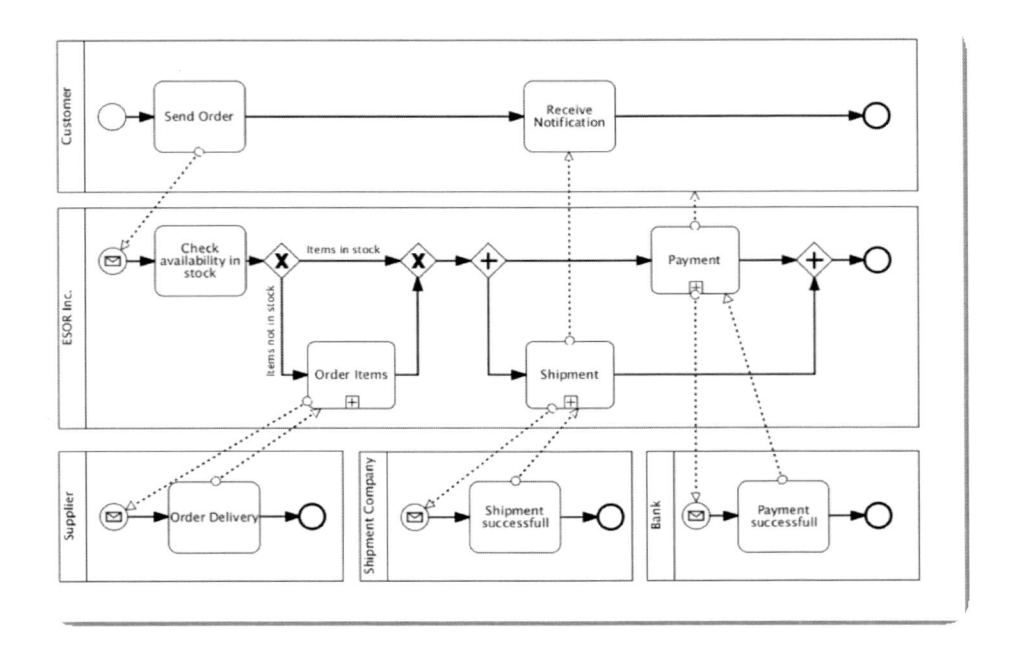

Figure 12 - BPMN Diagram of the underlying business-process

4.2 Defining properties of the KEI Framework

After specifying the context of this case study it is possible to identify requirements made to the KEI Framework. For this endeavor it is mandatory to identify the designated target or what should be achieved through building this information system for environmental data. The main goal is to strategically optimize processes based on their environmental impact. One must realize which environmental data is needed and have to be acquired. KEIs are a measure of the current business situation that is tied strategy by setting target values, like the definition in section 3.1 has been shown. Therefore one requirement is to gather the current environmental impact of the business-process. Through an energy and substance flux analysis interfaces of ESORs ordering-process to the environment will be identified. These substances and energies are gathered by monitoring the business-process, realized by the "information system" module of environmental-accounting. This makes it mandatory to think about how to monitor the business-process and get environmental information about it in an automatic manner. As a result, it is a requirement gathering substances and energies used by the process automatically and to store this data for analysis. Additionally it should be possible to define indicators and calculate these out of the persisted data. As the existing infrastructure does already calculate one KPI (Activity Duration on activity-instance level) the framework should be capable to persist them, too. Further target values for those indicators must be settable, as the definition of KEIs requires a target value to ensure connection to strategy.

Moreover it is planned to expand this KEI framework to other business-processes and should be flexible for expansion. If ESOR wants to manufacture their own products they need data about the used materials by the production process. It should be possible to expand the measurement system by this data and save it in the Datawarehouse.

As a result the main requirement to this project is flexibility for recording and persisting environmental relevant information concerning business-processes, as well as to define different indicators for activity-instances, activities, process-instances and processes.

Another requirement is to visualize this information in some way to provide a decision support system that enables to optimize business-processes.

Performance of the analysis is not primary for this work. But later on there are different possibilities to increase analysis performance later. Examples for increasing analysis performance are better hardware, saving pre-aggregated data in the Datawarehouse or developing a star- and/or snowflake schema, which would increase performance by violating the third normal form defined for databases.[133] Security aspects are not considered yet and are not set as a requirement.

Based on these requirements it comes to the selection of KEIs, which are going to be calculated for ESOR. This includes defining a strategy, deriving overall objectives out of strategy, executing substance- and energy flux analysis, thinking about a way to express environmental impact of the business-process and discussing target-values, which indicate the strategic desired situation.

---

[133] Cf. Heuer, A. et al. (2008), p.638ff.

4.3 Selection of processes-based KEIs

Now it comes to the practical selection of KEIs for ESOR. Therefore step one "define KEIs" of Figure 1 will be executed. To select concrete KEIs on the process level it is necessary to have a strategy, derive overall and specific objectives and operationalize them by identifying and implementing KEIs that measure the actual business situation. Further the requirements made to KEIs should also be considered.

As discussed in the theoretical determination of KEIs there are two possible approaches available for identifying KEIs. ESOR does not already measure environmental information and so it must be commenced with a top-down determination of KEIs beginning with the definition of ESORs strategy. In Figure 13 an extract of the strategy is illustrated. It is representing the "ambition" module of environmental-accounting. The vision that determines the strategy of ESOR is "to become the world's best online reseller". To follow this vision one strategy is to become sustainable. The sustainability strategy contains the aspects ecology and economy. Society, like the sustainability triangle defined, is not considered in this case study.

It is mandatory to reduce humanities' environmental impact wherever possible to ensure environmental health. ESOR realized its own responsibility to contribute ensuring environmental health and sustainable development as it has the realistic hierarchy of systems in mind (see section 2.2).

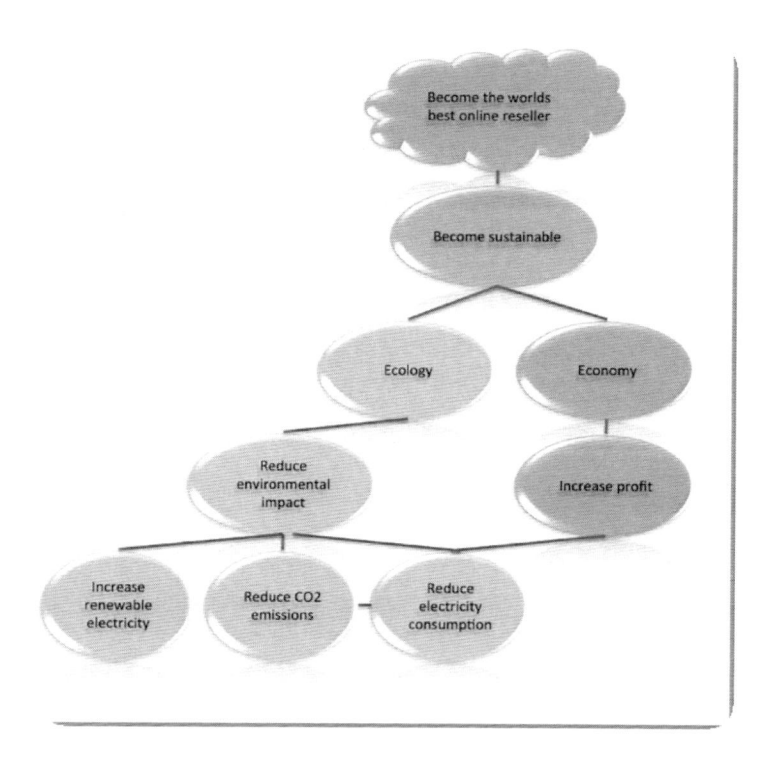

Figure 13 - Extract of ESORs Strategy

The overall objective is "reduce environmental impact". This is done by three specific objectives. First "increase amount of renewable electricity", following the substitution principle mentioned in section 3.5. Second "reduce carbon dioxide emissions" and third "reduce electricity consumption", which would contribute to the adaption principle. Through the reduction of electricity consumption, carbon dioxide emission and cost for electricity are decreased. Therefore it contributes to the economical goal "increase profits" of sustainability. Because of the fact that no artificial-based KEIs are going to be calculated the three objectives made to reduce environmental impact are going to be expressed as a KEI and not aggregated to environmental impact itself. To follow this overall objective ESOR has to pursue it on the different abstraction levels that are illustrated in Figure 7. As the purpose of this work is to optimize processes these specific objectives will be operationalized within the processes level of KEIs. Moreover processes have further levels. As they want to optimize their ordering-process

KEIs will be selected on process level and not further specified for process-instance, activities or activity-instances. Hereafter the overall objectives and level of abstraction ESOR defines the following resource-based KEIs:

- Average electricity consumption per process
- Average carbon dioxide emissions per process
- Percentage of clean electricity used per process
- Absolute electricity consumption per process
- Absolute clean electricity used per process
- Absolute carbon dioxide emission per process

Moreover to insure the "increase profit" objective, ESOR wants information about the average and absolute electricity costs. This can actually be identified as a monetary-based KEI or a KPI. It is identified as a KPI cause it is not used to aggregate energies with different scales of unit and not connected to the objective "to reduce environmental impact".

After KEIs for ESOR are selected it is necessary to identify environmental impacts that the ordering-process has. This procedure was stated as substance and energy flux analysis. It determines all energies and substances used by the ordering-process that causes impact on the environment. The defined ordering-process that was introduced in section 4.1, will be analyzed by the following analysis.

External partners (e.g. suppliers, shipment service providers or financial service providers) execute activities of this process. Because ESOR follows a full determination of energies and substances this analysis does include substances and energies used and ejected by purchased stuff and external partners.

The financial service provider would primarily use electricity for providing their service and depending on the energy mix it would cause carbon dioxide emissions or atomic waste. The suppliers and shipment service providers additionally use fuel for transportation, resulting in emission of carbon dioxide, too.

ESOR wants to manage and exchange their external partners based on the carbon dioxide emissions they caused at. It is the only substance connected to their specific objectives. Fuel and electricity are not considered, as they are not strategically relevant and contained in the emission of carbon dioxide.

To get external information about indirect emissions ESOR should has to ask its partners. Partners would need an environmental management system or at least gather this data to provide it to ESOR. So this case study assumes that this information is available to the external partners and they are also willing or forced to forward it to ESOR.

After identifying indirect emissions it comes to the internal activity "check availability in stock". It uses primarily electricity, which causes the emission of carbon dioxide as well as atomic waste, depending on the energy mix of the purchased electricity. So ESOR needs a means to measure the electricity consumption of its internal activities and a procedure to calculate how much carbon dioxide and atomic waste is ejected by it. Moreover the external activities are also executed in the business-process execution engine and used electricity.

The warehouse that ESOR owns and uses for storing products would be categorized under the product classification and not to the process class of KEIs, resulting in disregard of its environmental impact for this case study.

As a result of energy and substance flux analysis the ordering-process interacts with nature by using electricity and fuel on the input side. But on the output side it ejects carbon dioxide and atomic waste. Thereby it selects the following substances and energies that will be measured:

- Input of electricity
- Output of carbon dioxide and atomic waste

Reconsidering the identified specific objectives the ejection of atomic waste is not connected to ESORs strategy and will not be measured and visualized as a KEI. But it is indirectly connected to the objective "increase renewable electricity". Nevertheless it will be gathered as an environmental indicator. The atomic wastes caused by electricity consumption of external partners is not considered in this case study because it is not connected to strategy and would need additional efforts to get these data from external partners.

4.4 Architecture

After discussing strategy, which covers the module "ambition", it comes to the architecture of the KEI framework for business-processes. That should realize the calculation of KEIs, as well as provide an approach to persist and visualize this information for optimization. The second and third step of Figure 1 will be executed sequentially ("establishment of a measurement system" and "deployment of a management dashboard system"). Like the micro-view has illustrated these steps are covered by two components of environmental-accounting. An "information system" for measuring and persisting environmental data and a "decision support system" that calculates indicators based on measured data and enables optimization of business-processes in regard of their environmental impact.

As ESOR already has an existing architecture for executing business-processes the phases "planning", "define", "implement and test" and "process execution" of the BPM lifecycle are already running. The business-process is executed in the business process execution engine Apache ODE (Orchestration Directory Engine) and is defined in Business Process Execution Language (BPEL). The single activities are implemented as Web Services. A pluggable framework expands Apache ODE for providing some monitoring services that do not gather environmental data. Moreover there is a Complex Event Processing (CEP) Engine that is connected to the pluggable framework. It calculates metrics based on incoming events. These contribute to the phase "monitoring" of the BPM lifecycle. ESOR uses Apache ActiveMQ to connect Apache ODE, the pluggable framework and the CEP Engine with each other by messaging infrastructure. The "monitoring" phase of the BPM lifecycle will be expanded by building an "information system" and the "analysis" phase is enabled by a "decision support system". Both are modules of environmental-accounting.

The KEI framework for business-processes is designed as a "hub-and-spoke" architecture illustrated in Figure 14. It gets different data from several systems (spokes), loads and transforms this data into the Datawarehouse (representing the hub) and finally can be represented in several dashboards (spokes), which are adjusted to the relevant authorities.

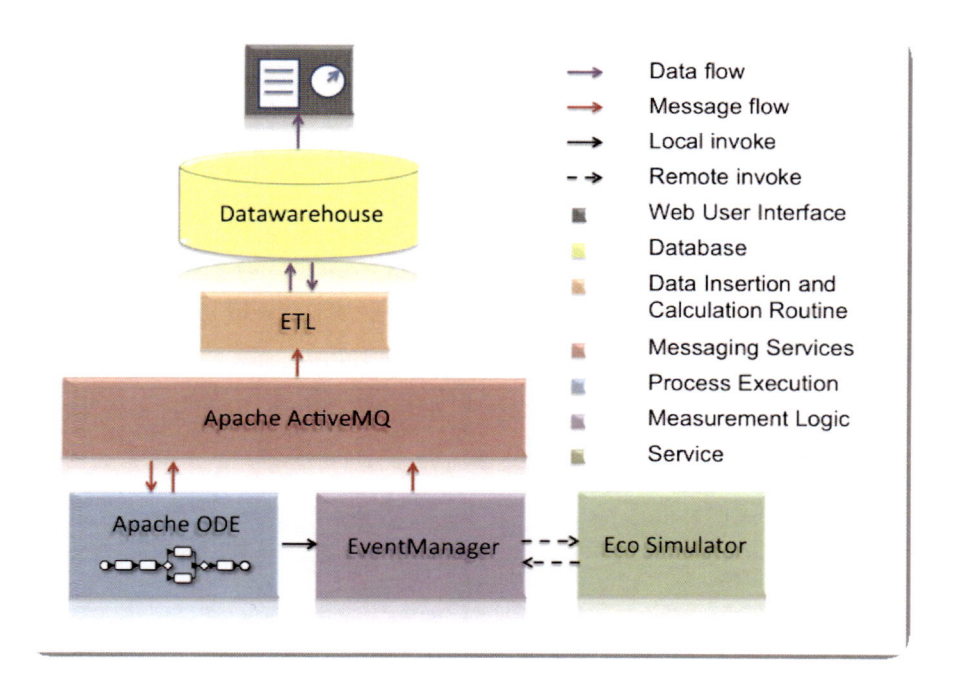

Figure 14 - General Architecture for KEI aware process execution

The components "Apache ODE" and "Apache ActiveMQ" represent the mentioned existing systems. The pluggable framework and CEP Engine are not visualized in the architecture, but it is assumed that they are included in Apache ODE. "EventManager" and "Eco Simulator" provide the monitoring function and measurement system for environmental impact, which is explained in sections 4.4.1 and 4.4.2. The Datawarehouse is the interface between the "monitor" and "analysis" phase. It enables to persist monitored events with their measured energies and substances for analysis. Moreover it contains the defined and calculated indicators and their corresponding target values. Thus it is the foundation for building dashboards, which are needed for the "analysis" phase of the BPM cycle. Several design choices for the Datawarehouse will be discussed and the concrete design will be shown in sections 4.4.3 and 4.4.4. The ETL-process extracts, transforms and loads the measured and monitored data into the Datawarehouse. This will be illustrated in section 4.4.5. The aggregation of data and calculation of KEIs could be executed in different ways, as well as the visualization in a dashboard are contents of sections 4.4.6 and 4.4.7 and represents the "decision support system".

4.4.1 Monitoring of process-execution

First it will be discussed how the "information system" can monitor the existing process-execution engine. The BPM cycle is assigned to the "monitoring" phase. Apache ODE, with its extension by pluggable framework produces events while deploying a business-process and during the execution of business-process-instances. In this case study the relevant events for monitoring environmental data are:

- Process deployment
- Process-Instance (start/end)
- Activity-Instance (start/end)

Actually the end of a process-instance or activity-instance is represented by two events. One occurs if the instance is executed properly and one if it has failed. The pluggable framework captures all events that are raised by Apache ODE and creates additional ones.

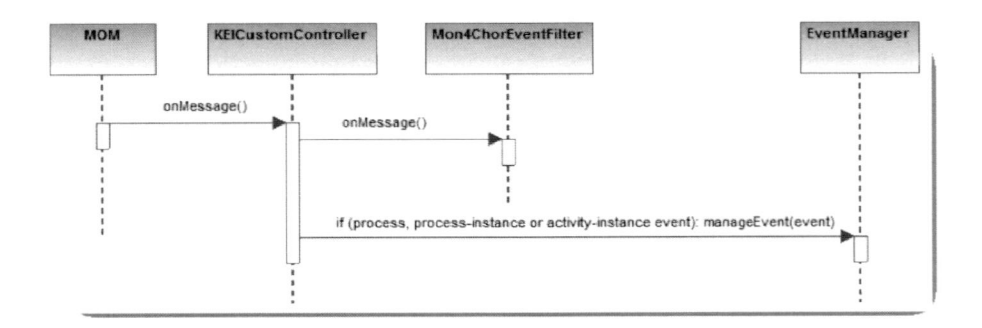

Figure 15 - Sequence Diagram - Event Capturing

It has a class named "KEICustomController", which includes a "onMessage()" method that will be invoked if events within ApacheODE occur. The abovementioned events are selected by the "KEICustomController" and are instantly forwarded to the "EventManager" calling its "manageEvent()" method. It also forwards events to the "Mon4ChronFilter" used by the CEP Engine to calculate metrics. This event capturing procedure is illustrated in the sequence diagram of Figure 15. It does visualize the selection of general events like process or process-instance events but not the detailed start and end events.

The "EventManager" handles all incoming events. The current implementation is monitoring environmental data based on activity-instances. Before figuring out how to measure substances and energies used, it will be shown how the "EventManager" handles process and process-instance events. Process events are forwarded without transformation straightaway to the MOMs "Operational Data Store (ODS) Queue". The ODS Queue represents the buffer that contains all event messages until they are actually loaded into the Datawarehouse. Process-instance events are not used to pre-aggregate data at the monitoring level, but it is a realistic option in some cases. The "EventManager" saves the start event and the correlation identifier provided by Apache ODE named "processID" (identifier for a process-instance) in a newly created "ProcessInstanceEvent" until the end event arrives and then passes this "ProcessInstanceEvent" containing those two events to the ODS Queue. The "ProcessInstanceEvents" not containing an "endEvent" are stored within the "EventManager" in a "LinkedList". If a process-instance end event occurs, it will be searched for a corresponding unfinished "ProcessInstanceEvent" by "correlationID". The "ProcessInstanceEvent" that was created and used by the "EventManager" is illustrated as a class diagram in Figure 16 and contains the created "ActivityInstanceEvent". This is needed for monitoring energies and substances in the next section.

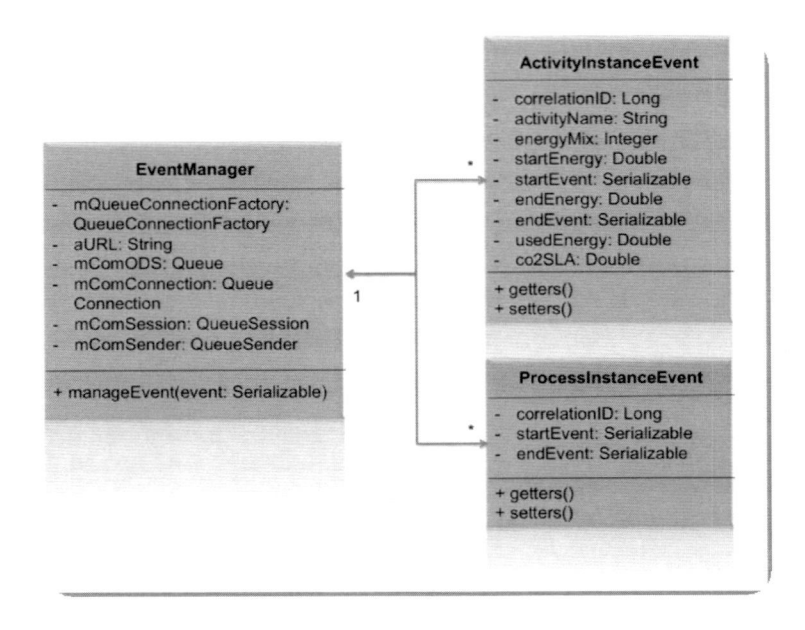

Figure 16 - Class diagram of defined Events for EventManager

With knowledge of how the "EventManager" gets the relevant events and handles events that are not used for measuring substances and energies an approach is needed that can handle activity-instance events.

4.4.2 Measurement of substances and energies

To measure energies and substances a means is needed to identify, which substances and energies are measured for a specific activity, enrich the corresponding activity-instance with this information and send it to the ODS Queue, where it can be inserted into the Datawarehouse by an ETL process. This is step two of Figure 1 "establish measurement system". It will expand monitoring of business-processes by environmental data, which are the identified substances and energies in section 4.3. These are needed to calculate KEIs.
This issue is solved by the components "EventManager" and "Eco Simulator" in the illustrated architecture of Figure 14.

The capturing of this data should be done in an automatic manner. It follows that the used resources or machinery for executing activity-instances of the business-process should be equipped with sensors that are capable capturing that information automatically.

The ordering-process is fictional and therefore it will be simulated. It results that no real sensors can be installed on existing resources. It leads to the solution to simulate sensors for the identified substances and energies. But how would carbon dioxide or atomic waste caused by consuming electricity measured in reality?

The power-supplier would actually cause it during the production of electricity. Therefore ESOR can't install sensors to gather this kind of data. Moreover it cannot be disregarded as carbon dioxide is connected to the sustainability strategy of ESOR and necessary to calculate the carbon dioxide KEI. Atomic waste should be gathered as it is defined as an environmental-indicator. Unfortunately external partners that perform the outsourced activities are simulated as well and don't provide data about the emission of carbon dioxide.

It results in three problems for the measurement of energies and substances that the ordering-process causes:

- Simulating electricity consumption
- Gathering emission of carbon dioxide and ejection of atomic waste
- Information about carbon dioxide emissions from outsourced activities of external partners

First it is started with the simulation of electricity consumption. Providing a random function that would create such a value is one possibility. It is an easy approach to simulate the consumption of electricity. But the simulated sensor should reflect reality. Therefore it will be implemented in a manner being more realistically and not only a simple random function.

When thinking about different kinds of sensors there are different possibilities how this data could be produced. A typical sensor, like a temperature sensor, would provide exactly one value per time that contains the actual temperature. It could be gathered by reading it. There is a research that expands such a sensor by WebService technology in a very low power-consuming way that enables to read it. A message or event can be send by the sensor if a certain value is exceeded or can be read actively by invoking a method.[134] This study proves that WebService sensors exists in a low power-consuming way and justifies why the "Eco Simulator" is implemented as a Web Service.

One possibility is to create a sensor measuring the actual power-consumption for a certain time period. It would get a start signal or event that will start the sensor to measure. The sensor will count the value by producing a random value every millisecond, second, or another period of time, until the activity ends and will tell the sensor to stop. The time for producing a random value depends on the required precision. Then all produced values will be added to gain the actual power-consumption of the activity-instance. This assumes that a sensor could be started and stopped like some kind of chronograph, which will be called a "push sensor", as it is only measuring a value if required. So with the starting event of an activity the sensor will be invoked to begin measuring, and invoked another time to stop. The disadvantage of this approach would be if activity-instances would run on the same resource concurrently. Therefore a sensor for each instance is needed, as it usually can't be started two times. Such a simulation approach was not chosen because it is very resource consuming by simulating a value every second and it is not the way power-consumption is actually measured in practice.

In fact to measure usage of electricity there is an electricity meter that counts the overall energy consumption of one resource or household. It will be stated as a "pull sensor", as it is constantly measuring something and can only be read. It would require reading the electricity meter once the activity has been started and once after it completed or faulted. Because of the reason that it failed it still consumed electricity during its execution. By subtracting the start value from the end value it is possible to calculate the amount of used electricity, which is the chosen approach to measure electricity-consumption of activity-instances. The implemented "Eco Simulator" is illustrated in a class diagram in Figure 17 and simulates the electricity meter by the method "simulateEnergy()".

---

[134] See Priyantha, N.B., et al. (2008)

It has three parameters: "firstEnergyCount", "activityDuration" and "maxValue". The "firstEnergyCount" parameter is used to ensure that the second read is bigger than the first one. "ActivityDuration" is used to simulate a value that depends on time an activity-instance needed to complete. The last parameter "maxValue" is needed to set a boundary for the range of simulated values.

```
EcoSimulator
────────────────
+ simulateEnergy(
    firstEnergyCount: Double,
    activityDuration: Long,
    maxValue: Integer)
+ simulateEnergyMix()
```

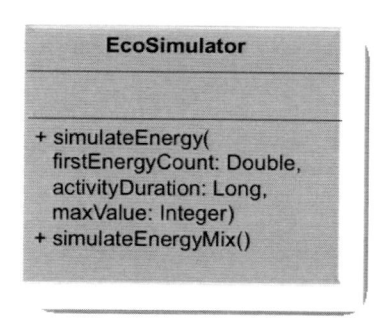

Figure 17 - Class Diagram EcoSimulator

There is a second method called "simulateEnergyMix()", which will be will be explained later. A concrete example and the procedure of simulating electricity consumption are shown in Figure 19 and Figure 20.

Even if activities are executed concurrently with this approach a component can be implemented that will be able to identify how many activities have been executed within the same period of time on the same resource and divide the electricity-consumption by the amount of activities. If the individual period of time of the activity-instances were not equal this would get complicated. Moreover another activity-instance might be started or completed during the interval so that a new amount of concurrent running activities for dividing power-consumption would have to be calculated every time a further activity-instance is executed on the resource. As Apache ODE does not provide information about the resource on which activity-instances have been executed the issue of concurrent running activity-instances on one resource will be ignored. Moreover the current implementation of the business-process does not support concurrent execution of process-instances. Therefore this assumption is permitted. Expanding the "EventManager" or developing a further component could solve this issue. It would manage and calculate the resource usage of one activity-instance and divide it by the quantity of activity-instances currently running on this resource. But there are further issues. If different activity-instances would run on the same computer concurrently they could use more or less CPU usage than other activity-instances and thus use more or less electricity. As a result it would not be precise dividing the power-consumption by the amount of concurrent running activity-instances. It follows that an exact and precise allocation to a certain activity-instance it is not easy achievable. The economical requirement made to KEIs can actually determine how precisely electricity usage is going to be measured, as the costs for accuracy should be proportional to the generated benefits.

To use this "pull sensor" approach, it is necessary to capture three events within the "EventManager" (see the previous section). These events enable to simulate power consumption and other energies and substances used or ejected by activity-instances. The "activity_executing" event indicates that an activity-instance has been started and will induce a first read of the electricity meter. To induce the second read from the electricity meter there are two events available. First "activity_executed", illustrates the activity-instance completed correctly. Second "activity_failed", indicates that it failed, but still would have used electricity as it is executed in Apache ODE.

The next issue that is to discuss is how carbon dioxide emission and atomic waste can be measured. Both are ejected by ESOR consuming electricity. It wouldn't be realistically to simulate this data by simulating a sensor that measures the emission and waste of an activity-instance by ESOR, as they are an ejection of emission and waste from "purchased stuff". They are emitted during the production of electricity at the power supplier where it could be measured by a sensor. As a consequence the only real possibility for ESOR to get this data is asking its power-suppliers for it. All electricity providers in Germany are obligated to publish information about composition of substances used for producing electricity, as well as about the corresponding environmental impact. It obligatorily has to include information about carbon dioxide emission and the amount of atomic waste.[135] This data could be used to calculate carbon dioxide emission and atomic waste ejection indirectly based on the consumption of electricity. As a corporation could have more than one electricity provider, and might be distributed in more than one country it is not recommended to statically annotate a certain activity or process by this information. Moreover the activity-instances of a business-process can be executed in different locations. It results in the solution that the "Eco Simulator" does simulate an Integer number by the method "simulateEnergyMix()" that will identify an electricity provider that was used for the execution of a single activity-instance.

This number will identify, which energy-mix was used and how much carbon dioxide and atomic waste is emitted per kW/h and how much the consumed electricity did cost. With this information the simulated electricity consumption can be transformed to emission of carbon dioxide, ejection of atomic waste and electricity costs. They are gathered by multiplying the simulated electricity consumption with the data about how much emission and waste were caused per kW/h.

Finally the problem of gathering carbon dioxide emissions of outsourced activities for external partners must be solved. ESOR cannot simply install sensors for getting this information, as the resources causing them are not belonging to them. This fact results in the solution to define some kind of Service Level Agreements that would contain the average emission of carbon dioxide that is caused per shipment or for the financial service provider per transaction to get environmental impact of these external activities. It should be mentioned that this leads to a certain imprecision, as this would probably not be the actual but an average value depending on the implemented environmental management system of the partner. As the partners are simulated, a fixed average value for emission of carbon dioxide will be assumed that was negotiated with the external partners by ESOR. This value could be used to simulate the actual carbon dioxide emission by the "Eco Simulator" and is assuming that the external partners do have an EMS that is capable to gather the actual emission for one

---

[135] § 42 | Abs.1 | S.1,2 EnWG

process-instance. The implemented KEI framework is assuming that only a static carbon dioxide SLA is available to ESOR. Nevertheless it is changeable by implementing a new method within the "Eco Simulator" that simulates a random value that is constraint to the negotiated SLA or could be set higher to include the simulation of SLA violations.

Now it is illustrated how the identified energies and substances of ESOR will be measured, the concept of the "EventManager" will be introduced. This was designed in terms of flexibility. The "EventManager" must be able to capture events of interest and a routine to identify, handle, simulate and gather ecological-data for the abovementioned aspects and in the end forward the created events to the ODS Queue, where it is stored until it is loaded and transformed into the Datawarehouse.

Section 4.4.1 has shown that the "EventManager" gets the relevant events by the "KEICustomController". First it has to distinguish incoming events as process, process-instance and activity-instance events. Unfortunately there are no events for activities, which results in a certain issue discussed in the ETL section. Process events will be forwarded instantly to the ODS Queue and process-instance events raised by Apache ODE are saved in a newly defined "ProcessInstanceEvent" (see Figure 16). These process and process-instance events are easy to handle as no environmental data will be simulated on this level, but the events on activity-instance level are the relevant ones. The "EventManager" need a means to identify to which process model the activity-instances belongs and which environmental information should be simulated for this kind of activity.

The first solution was very static and hard coded in the "EventManager". It simply checked the process name that indicates the process an activity-instance belongs to. Afterwards it distinguished activity-instances by its xpath. Next it invoked the "Eco Simulator" if electricity should be simulated and/or statically contained a carbon dioxide emission SLA. But this hardcoded approach is too inflexible, because the code of the "EventManager" has to be changed anytime a further process will be monitored or an existing definition will alter. Therefore another approach was needed.

The identification logic and the definition which environmental data should be simulated must be "outsourced" in some way to avoid this hard coded approach. To outsource the identification and definition logic there are several opportunities available like a text file, a database or an xml file. Xml was chosen, as it is very wide spread. It provides the ability to structure a document and does not need further products to install.

```xml
<processes>
    <process>
        <name>{http://iaas.uni-stuttgart.de/purchaseOrder/resellerProcess}PurchaseOrderResellerProcess</name>
        <activities>
            <activity>
                <name>check availability in stock</name>
                <xpath>/process/sequence[1]/sequence[1]/repeatUntil[1]/sequence[1]/invoke[1]</xpath>
                <simulation>
                    <energy>true</energy>
                    <co2sla>false</co2sla>
                </simulation>
            </activity>
            <activity>
                <name>orderItemFromSupplier1</name>
                <xpath>/process/sequence[1]/if[1]/sequence[1]/repeatUntil[1]/sequence[1]/invoke[1]</xpath>
                <simulation>
                    <energy>true</energy>
                    <co2sla>22.0</co2sla>
                </simulation>
            </activity>
```

Figure 18 - ConfigManager File

Within the xml file one can define processes that are defined by its qualified name. Every process has several activities that are identified by xpath and an activity name is included. This is helpful for visualization and Apache ODE does unfortunately not provide this data. For each activity it will be defined, which environmental data is going to be simulated, as well as the negotiated carbon dioxide SLA for activities executed by external partners. The "EventManager" loads the "configManager.xml" file and checks whether there is a simulation definition or SLA for the activity-instance event that should be handled. If events occur that the "EventManager" cannot identify by process-name and activity-xpath, it will report this fact on the console and show the affected process-name and xpath.

Depending on the environmental data that is going to be simulated. The "EventManager" will start the simulation of this data or read the defined SLA. As ESOR does only consume electricity it is the only simulation that takes place. But the "EventManager" can be expanded by new simulation definitions in the "configManager.xml" file illustrated in Figure 18. Afterwards a routine would have to be added to the "EventManager" that defines how to gather or simulate this data.

In Figure 19 an example is illustrated how the implemented "EventManager" functions if it should simulate electricity consumption. First it gets the "activity_executing" event from the "KEICustomController" calling its "manageEvent()" method (1.). Within this event Apache ODE provides the process-name and activity-xpath, which are needed to identify the activity. With this data the "EventManager" checks its configManager.xml file to determine if electricity should be simulated (2.). If this is the case the "EventManager" invokes the "Eco Simulator" to simulate a read from an electricity meter (3.). After getting the first electricity consumption value (4.) it creates an "ActivityInstanceEvent" (illustrated in Figure 16) that has a "correlationID" attribute that is the "activityID" (identifying an activity-instance) generated by Apache ODE. Moreover an "ActivityInstanceEvent" consists of the attributes "startEnergy", "endEnergy", "co2SLA", "energyMix", "activityName", "calculatedEnergy" and the original "startEvent" and "endEvent". After setting the correlation ID it will set the original start message and then the simulated start energy value as well as the energy-mix ID that was simulated, too. This new event is saved in the internal activity-list (5.). If the activity executed or the failed event occurred (6.) this event will also be looked up in configManager.xml to identify what should be simulated (7.). Then it takes its "activityID" to search in the activity-list for its corresponding start Event (8.). With this information it is possible to invoke the "Eco Simulator" in a way that it generates a bigger value than the first one (9.). This information (10.) and the end event are saved in the activity-instance event of the "EventManager" (11.). Afterwards it will be sent to the "buffer" (12.) and deleted from the ActivityList (13.).

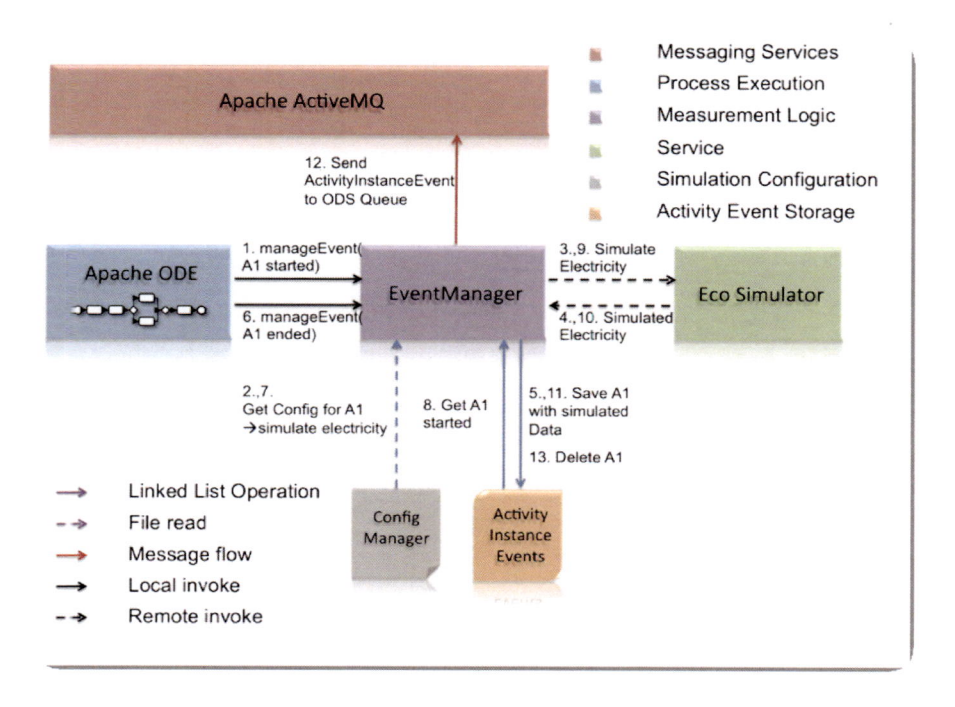

Figure 19 - Functioning of EventManager simulating energy data

This electricity simulating procedure is also illustrated in Figure 20 as a sequence diagram. It contains the interaction between the different classes used for simulation. A certain aspect should be mentioned concerning the invocation of the "simulateEnergy()" method of the EcoSimulator. The "maxValue" for simulating electricity start value has been statically set to 4000 W/h, the "activityDuration" to one as it is used for multiplication and the "firstEnergyValue" is set to zero. For simulating the end value "maxValue" is statically set to 8000 W/h, "activityDuration" is calculated by the timestamps of start- and end event and the "firstEnergyValue" is the value simulated for the corresponding start event.

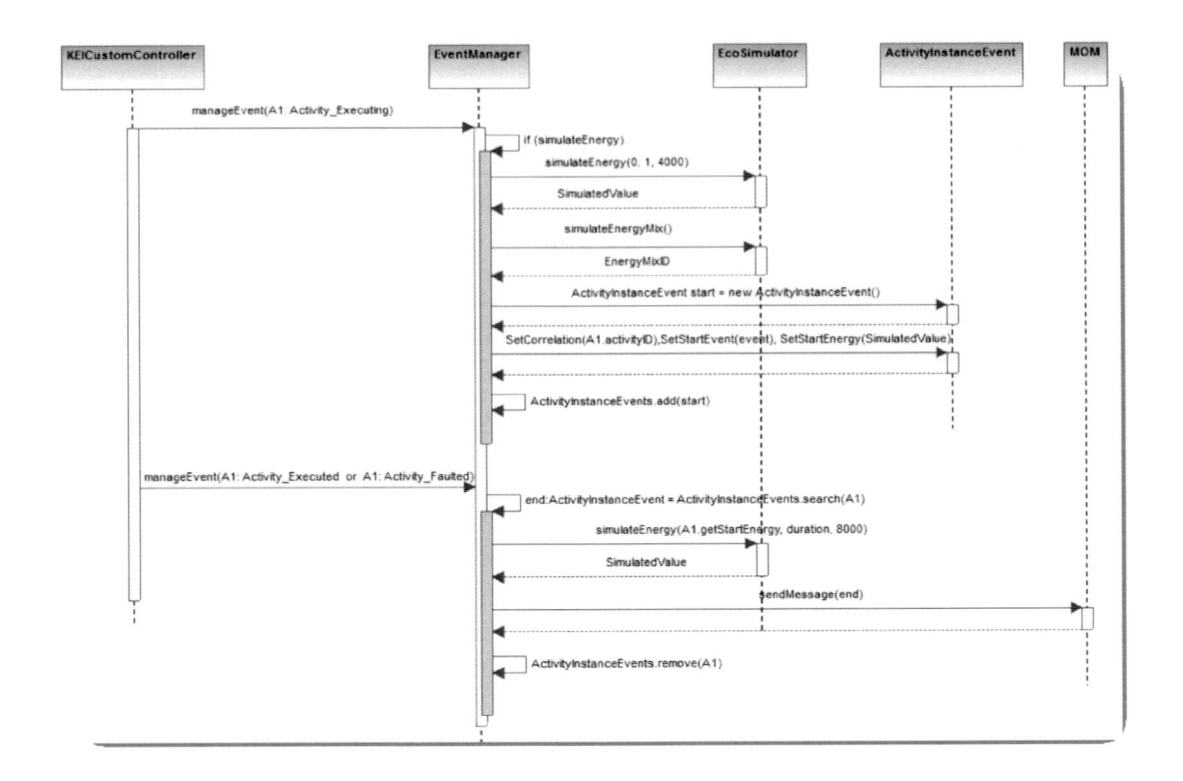

Figure 20 - Sequence Diagram EventManager

The procedure for the external activities that have a carbon dioxide SLA is similar. The "Eco Simulator" part is not used but the value within the "configManager.xml" is read and set for the "ActivityInstanceEvent".

The emission of carbon dioxide and ejection of atomic waste could be calculated by the "EventManager". This would require access to the energy-mix data included in the Datawarehouse. This transformation is done by the ETL process to separate actual measuring from transformation routines.

Finally a certain observation should be mentioned in terms of reliability. If the "EventManager" crashes the internally stored "ActivityInstanceEvents" and "ProcessInstanceEvents" these would be lost. It would result in incomplete monitoring information. In terms of reliability they should be altered to a database or other mechanism that would not lose those instances if a crash would occur.

With this fundamental structure to monitor business-processes by its used and ejected substances and energies the "information system" module of environmental-accounting is almost implemented and "monitoring" phase of the BPM lifecycle is enabled. This monitored data should be persisted for the "decision support system" and "analysis" phase. In the following it comes to the Datawarehouse design.

4.4.3 Granularity of data

Before defining the Datawarehouse-schema it is mandatory to think about another design choice that has a major impact on the design of the Datawarehouse as well as on the economical requirement made to KEIs. That choice is granularity of data and will determine which data will be saved. It is probably one of the most important and hardest decisions that have to be made if building a Datawarehouse.[136]

Granularity decides which aspects can be analyzed and which ones not. It additionally affects the volume of data that resides in the data warehouse and the type of queries that can be answered. To avoid misunderstandings a short explanation of granularity will be given. Granularity refers to the level of detail or summarization of units of data in the Datawarehouse. The more detail there is, the lower the level of granularity. The less detail there is, the higher the level of granularity.[137]

The previously introduced measurement of substances and energies is actually done on a very low level of granularity, as it is based on activity-instances. This is the most detailed information that is available for business-processes. Granularity defines if each activity-instance and its environmental impact are persisted individually or if it is aggregated to activity, process-instance or process level and then stored in the Datawarehouse. Aggregation to activity level would mean that within the analysis it could not be identified if certain activity-instances caused higher electricity consumption. Higher granularity requires less storage

---

[136] Cf. Inmon, W.H. (2005), p.41.
[137] Cf. Inmon, W.H. (2005), p.41.

capacity and decreases the profitability aspect of the economical requirement. As flexibility is the most important requirement to this KEI framework and the lower the level of granularity, the better the flexibility and the poorer the performance, the level of granularity will be set on activity-instance level.

4.4.4 Datawarehouse Design

After setting granularity of data on activity-instance level, it is possible to design a schema for the Datawarehouse, which will be used for later visualization and analysis. As ESOR wants to gather environmentally relevant information to manage business-processes the single aspects of the processes should be realized in the Datawarehouse model. They are needed to distinguish the different classes of KEIs defined for the processes category. Reconsidering the flexibility requirement the Datawarehouse does determine which information can be persisted and is available for later analysis. Moreover it should be flexible enough to be used by other companies and business-processes to calculate KEIs, so it has a major influence on the flexibility of this framework. It is fundamental for the "information system" and "decision support system" module of environmental accounting and enables "monitoring" and "analysis" phase of the BPM lifecycle. The following aspects have to be considered and modeled in the DW:

- Persisting of process-execution
- Date and time dependency
- Energy and substance flux analysis
- Measuring energies and substances
- Transformation from electricity usage to emission and waste
- Persisting indicators and target values

The realized Datawarehouse schema for this KEI Framework is completely illustrated in Figure 21 by an Entity Relationship Model (ERM). The attributes, primary keys and foreign keys of the created tables are shown in Figure 22. In the following the above-mentioned aspects will be explained sequentially.

Beginning with the explanation of the basic tables that enable to persist the occurring processes, process-instances, activities and activity-instances. These are four different entities and they will be modeled in four tables named "process", "activity", "process-instance" and "activity-instance". For each process start event like the order of a customer, a separate process instance from an existing process-definition will be created in the business process execution engine. t results in the connection from table process to process-instance.

A process contains zero or more process-instances that are derived from it and one process-instance is assigned to exactly one process. Each business-process contains one or more activities in its definition, which are the steps that take place to execute the process and are performed in a predefined sequence. This implies that for each process-instance an instance for each activity will be generated. Each process-instance has one or more activity-instances associated to it, but every activity-instance is assigned to exactly one process-instance. From each activity zero or more activity-instances are derived, but every activity-instance is assigned to exactly one activity.

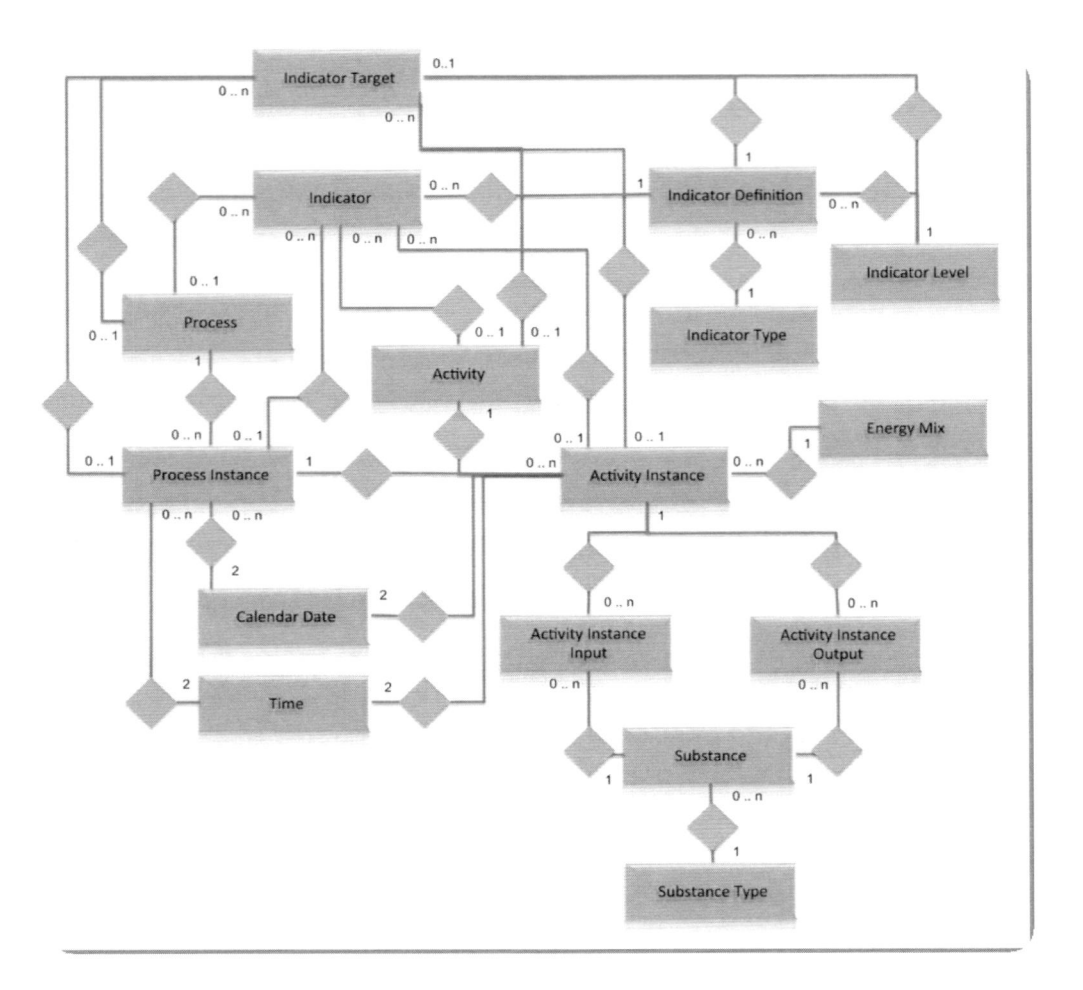

Figure 21 - Datawarehouse ERM

A certain issue is that an activity is only indirectly connected to a process because it could be used in more than one process definition. Otherwise another table would be needed that contains the relation from process to activity to ensure third normal form. But as this connection is not primary for the KEI framework this table is not created. Another option was to add the qualified process-name as a foreign key to activity-instances and activities, which would lead to a better aggregation performance but higher storage capacity. This option is useful for developing a Star- or Snowflake schema that enables aggregation to process-level directly on activity-instance-level without joining the tables "activity-instance", "process-instance" and "process".

Activity (activity_id, xpath, activity_name)
ActivityInstance (activityinstance_id, processinstance_id, xpath, State_Active_Time_Key, State_Active_Date_Key, State_Ended_Time_Key, State_Ended_Date_Key, energy_mix_id)
Activityinstance_Input (ai_input_id, activityinstance_id, substance_id, substance_amount)
Activityinstance_Output (ai_output_id, activityinstance_id, substance_id, substance_amount)
Calendar_Date (Calendar_Date_Key, Day, Month, Year, Day_of_Week, Day_Number_Of_Week, Day_Number_Of_Month, Day_Number_In_Year, Week_Number_In_Month, Week_Number_In_Year, Quarter_Number_In_Year)
Energy_mix (energy_mix_id, fossil_fuels, nuclear_power, clean_energy, price_kwh_in_EUR, co2_emission_in_g_kwh, atomic_waste_in_mg_kwh)
Indicator (indicator_id, indicatordefinition_id, correlation_id, indicator_value)
Indicator_definition (indicatordefinition_id, indicator_type_id, indicatorlevel_id, indicatordefinition_name, scale_unit, calculation_description)
Indicator_level (indicatorlevel_id, level_name)
Indicator_target (target_id, indicatordefinition_id, indicatorlevel_id, correlation_id, target_value)
Indicator_type (indicator_type_id, indicator_type)
Process (process_id, process_version, process_name, process_timestamp, bpel_process)
ProcessInstance (processinstance_id, process_name, State_Active_Time_Key, State_Active_Date_Key, State_Ended_Time_Key, State_Ended_Date_Key)
Substance (substance_id, substance_name, scaleUnit, loading, substance_type_id)
Substance_type (substance_type_id, substance_type_name)
Time (Time_Key, Hour, Minutes, Seconds)

Figure 22 - Relationship Schema

Moreover one should think about the primary keys that enable identification of exactly one dataset. In the illustrated relationship schema the primary keys are underlined solid and the foreign keys are underlined dotted. Actually Apache ODE provides a qualified name for processes and is unique for identification; nonetheless the database additionally creates an auto incremented ID anytime a new process is inserted into the Datawarehouse, as the chosen database does not support primary keys defined as a text field. Additionally this newly created numeric key is needed to solve an issue that occurred during the design of the indicator tables, which will be discussed later. Besides the primary key the process table also contains the field "bpel_file". It was created for the "decision support system" enabling "analysis" phase of the BPM lifecycle. Process-instances and activity-instances use the primary key generated by Apache

ODE, as it is a numeric ID. Activities are identified by xpath, but the same problematic would occur, as it would be a primary key based on text so the database creates an auto incremented ID for it as well.

This is the fundamental structure to model and save data about business-process execution in the Datawarehouse.

It leads to the next issue, time and date dependency. As process-instances and activity-instances are actually executed they have a time and date dependency and thus are connected to the tables "calendar date" and "time". The process table also has a certain time and date dependency, but this is included in the qualified name by Apache ODE that changes if the process-definition alters. It is indirectly considered and will not have a connection to those two tables. Each process- and activity-instance is connected to exactly two calendar date and time entries. One is indicating the starting point or the point in time when execution was started and one contains the end point when the activity was executed completely or failed. A certain date or time could be connected to zero or more process-instances or activity-instances. Zero results because of the fact that one time entry could only be connected to a process-instance and not to an activity-instance and vice versa. Another option to add date and time dependency was to add two timestamp fields into the process- and activity-instance tables. One indicating its start time and one its end time, but this would harm the third normal form and thus store redundant information. It results in more required storage capacity. This option was not chosen because it requires more storage capacity. The process table actually has a timestamp included to be more flexible in case the business-process execution engine that is used would not provide a qualified name, which would alter if the business-process changes. One might raise an objection that this would also harm the third normal form, but the process table does not contain as much data entries as the both instance tables this violation is permitted.

The primary key for date and time tables is an auto-generated key that is created by the database and added to process- and activity-instance tables as foreign key to identify date and time of execution.

As a result the fundamental structure was expanded by time information. These are necessary to identify instances or a set of activity- and process-instances for calculating KEIs that match the individual definition of the current business situation. It was a period of time from past to today that represented the current business situation (see section 3.1).

As ESOR defined the current situation as since the last business-process change this time and date tables are not really needed in this case study. The current situation is represented in the qualified process name that changes if the business-process definition does change. So they are not relevant for the calculation of ESORs KEIs.

Next the structure to persist the results of energy- and substance flux analysis will be discussed. As it could contain a huge variety of different energies and substances a means is needed that provides to define substances and energies that are actually used and afterwards can be used to measure inputs and outputs of activity-instances.

The first design defined a table for each class of substances like material, energy, waste and emission. This caused a certain problem, because substances that are used as material could also be substances that are ejected as waste. Additionally if a new category is identified or the specified categories would change the structure of the Datawarehouse would have to be changed, too. It follows that the Datawarehouse would not be conform to the third normal form, substances might have to be defined several times for different categories and is not that flexible to category changes.

It led to the solution to create a "substance" and "substance type" table. The "substance type" defines the category of the "substance", like material, emission, waste, etc. A certain naming issue should be mentioned, as actually the table name "substance" contains energies, too.

The "substance types" that were identified are illustrated in Figure 23. The four identified interfaces of Figure 4 in section 2.3 and the categories of substances and energies shown in section 3.5 were used to identify different types of substances. The following categories were selected: energy, material, emission, waste, land and product. Land, material and product are momentarily not used, but if ESOR would manufacture products they could be useful to identify additional data about environmental impact.

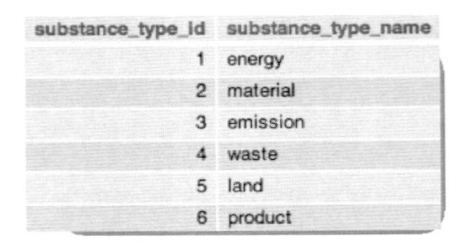

substance_type_id	substance_type_name
1	energy
2	material
3	emission
4	waste
5	land
6	product

Figure 23 - Table Substance Type

This design is a flexible approach to identify, separate and categorize different kinds of substances.

Within the table "substance" the actual substances and energies used are defined and their applied scale of unit. Each "substance" is connected to exactly one "substance type". This modeling approach causes the issue that a substance occurring in more than one category would have to be defined several times. But the definition of categories is flexible so that a new category could be created for example "material and emission" if a substance is used in both categories or creating a substance for each category to solve this problem. Thus no further table is introduced to model relation to more than one substance type. The "substance type" table is actually not used in this case study, but has been created to aggregate substances to substance types.

As a result this manner is flexible to persist the results of the energy and substance flux analysis and is also usable for calculating resource-based or artificial-based KEIs containing more than one substance. The results of the energy and substance flux analysis of ESOR executed in section 4.3 and are visualized in Figure 24. Electricity is categorized as "energy", carbon dioxide as "emission" and atomic waste as "waste". It additionally provides a field called "loading" that is designated for artificial-based KEIs like the mentioned ecological footprint, or to aggregate substances with the same scale of unit to resource-based KEIs. But as no artificial-indicators were selected, nor substances with the same scale of unit are aggregated to resources-based KEIs it is not that relevant for this case study. Therefore it is set to one for each substance. Nonetheless if artificial-based KEIs should be calculated the Datawarehouse provides a means to set a loading-factor to build and calculate those sorts of KEIs. Another thought was to add a loading factor to the substance type table, but it is questionable if emissions could be aggregated with materials, which has been discussed in the section "Determination of KEIs", this attribute was not created. But it could be easily added if an approach will be developed to aggregate all kinds of environmental impacts.

substance_id	substance_name	scaleUnit	loading	substance_type_id
1	electricity	W/h	1.0000	1
2	carbon dioxide	g	1.0000	3
3	atomic waste	mg	1.0000	4

Figure 24 - Table Substance

After modeling how to store results of energy and substance flux analysis, an approach is needed to persist the measured values of those substances for all activity-instances.

The previous section about granularity of data illustrated that measuring and persisting environmental data on activity-instance level provides the most flexibility for queries and analysis. As flexibility was a fundamental requirement, the Datawarehouse must be capable to persist this data on activity-instance level. Thus a connection between substances and activity-instances is needed. It can be aggregated, as it is connected to the "activity" and "process-instance" table, which is again related to the "process" table. Therefore environmental data is connected to the "activity-instance" table and can be aggregated to each process level, which provides the most flexibility.

To separate the interfaces to ecology each activity-instance has zero or more "ActivityInstance_Inputs" and "ActivityInstance_Outputs" associated. These are connected to exactly one substance. This enables the possibility to identify the same substance as an input and output of an activity-instance. Both primary keys are generated by the database and contain a field "substance amount" that contains the monitored value for a substance. Moreover KEIs can also be distinguished, whether they are an input or output of an activity-instance.

The issue to transform the input of electricity to the output of carbon dioxide and atomic waste is solved by simulating an energy-mix-ID, which identifies the power-supplier that was used for executing this activity. Therefore the table "energy mix" has been created. It stores the energy-mixes of the power-suppliers from which a company orders their electricity. Figure 25 illustrates this table with its contained information, like the constellation of electricity divided in fossil fuels, nuclear power and clean energy in percent, as well as information about the costs of electricity, emission of carbon dioxide and ejection of atomic waste. This table makes it possible to calculate the outputs carbon dioxide and atomic waste of an activity-instance, as well as the electricity costs it caused. Additionally it is needed to calculate the KEI percentage of clean electricity. Therefore it contains the three columns "fossil_fuel", "nuclear_power" and "clean_energy". The value is a percentage value and adding all three values should result in the value "100".

fossil_fuels	nuclear_power	clean_energy	price_kwh_in_EUR	co2_emission_in_g_kwh	atomic_waste_in_mg_kwh
66	19	15	0.210	500.00	0.90
61	17	22	0.250	681.00	0.50
24	47	24	0.230	235.00	1.30
0	0	100	0.270	0.00	0.00

Figure 25 - Table Energy Mix

ESOR identified four power providers with different electricity constellations and ejection of waste and emission. The table also contains an energy-mix-ID that is not illustrated in the figure, but is actually the value that is simulated for an activity-instance and provides the relation to transform the electricity consumption to the corresponding activity-instance outputs. So an activity-instance is connected to exactly one energy-mix and one energy-mix is connected to zero or more activity-instances.

Next the structure for defining and persisting calculated indicators is going to be shown. This was a very hard endeavor as there could be defined several kinds of indicators on different aggregation levels like indicators on activity-instance, process-instance, activity or process level. In terms of flexibility all of them should be storable in the Datawarehouse and in terms of performance to provide the option of persisting pre-aggregated and calculated indicators.

A first table has been created to identify different types of indicators, named "Indicator Type", which is illustrated in Figure 26.

indicator_type_id	indicator_type
1	KEI
2	KPI
3	Indicator
4	Environmental Indicator

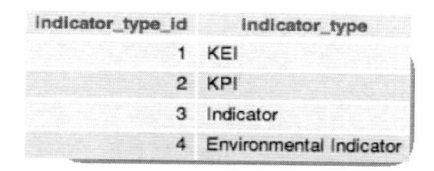

Figure 26 - Table Indicator Types

It defines the following kinds of indicators: indicator, environmental indicator, KPI and KEI (identified and discussed in section 3.1). So the Datawarehouse can persist and separate different kinds of indicators for analysis and not just KEIs.

The next design choice about the level of an indicator, such as process or process-instance, has been very difficult.

The very first design assumed that indicators are only stored on activity-instance basis and aggregated anytime a dashboard invokes a query. By this assumption flexibility would be decreased, because one is constraint to define and persist activity-instance indicators in the DW. As a result the indicator calculation logic would be included to the dashboard and every time an indicator on process-level is needed it would has to be aggregated again. This is a performance aspect, but by using this approach only pre-calculated indicators could be provided on activity-instance level. Moreover this depends on the economical requirement made to KEIs. To aggregate indicators on a higher level of abstraction any time a request is made by the dashboard would need a better IT-infrastructure. This is more expensive but would improve the time aspect of the economical requirement, as the indicator would include the newest information, if the monitoring data were instantly inserted into the Datawarehouse. So actually the concrete decision which levels are pre-aggregated depends on the individual requirements that a corporation has concerning the aspects time and profitability. But as the requirement to this framework is flexibility the DW should provide the possibility to persist pre-aggregated data on each level.

These arguments led to another approach, defining two tables: "process-indicators" and "activity-instance indicators". It enabled the Datawarehouse to provide pre-aggregated indicators on process level, as these give a good overview of the environmental impact and performance of one business-process and decreases traffic to the Datawarehouse. Unfortunately it also limits flexibility to define pre-aggregated indicators as no activity or process-instance indicators can be persisted in the DW.

Further it is needed to identify indicators on all levels. The solution to create a table for each level was too redundant, as the only differentiation of the tables would be the correlation ID and no additional abstraction levels, like all processes, are definable without adding new tables.

indicatorlevel_Id	level_name
1	Process
2	Activity
3	Activity-Instance
4	Process-Instance

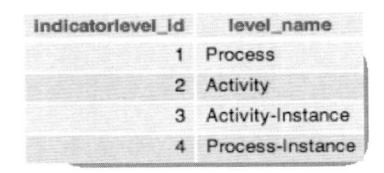

Figure 27 - Table Indicator Level

To provide this flexibility the first table created is called "indicator level" and is illustrated in Figure 27. It is used to differentiate indicators on their level of abstraction. The fundamental structure of business-processes contained four different entities. This table includes an entry for each of them to provide the most flexibility to persist pre-aggregated indicators and follows the "processes" classification of KEIs discussed in section 3.3.

Afterwards a means is needed to define indicators and persist their value. An indicator could be used for more than one process-model and therefore it is necessary to separate the concrete value from the definition table. Because if they would be stored in one table it is violating the third normal form and implies that an ndicator must be defined anytime a value was calculated for another process. With two separate tables it is possible to define indicators independent from the calculated value and it provides the better flexibility.

indicatordefinition_id	indicator_type_id	indicatorlevel_id	indicatordefinition_name	scale_unit	calculation_description
1	1	3	Electricity Usage	W/h	
2	1	3	Co2 Emission	g	
3	1	3	Clean Energy	W/h	
4	2	3	Electricity Costs	EUR	
5	4	3	Atomic Waste	mg	
6	1	1	Average Electricity Consumption	W/h	
7	2	1	Average Electricity Costs	EUR	
8	1	1	Average Co2 Emission	g	
9	4	1	Average Atomic Waste	mg	
10	1	1	Percentage Clean Energy	%	
11	1	1	Absolute Electricity Consumption	W/h	
12	1	1	Absolute Co2 Emission	g	
13	1	1	Absolute Clean Energy	W/h	
14	2	1	Absolute Electricity Costs	EUR	
15	4	1	Absolute Atomic Waste	mg	
16	2	3	Activity Duration	sec	

Figure 28 - Table Indicator Definition

Starting with the realized "indicator definition" table, which defines the "indicatordefinition_name", its scale of unit, the type and level of indicator, which were introduced before, as well as the opportunity to describe how the indicator is calculated to ensure transparency. In Figure 28 the defined indicators of ESOR are illustrated, including the selected KEIs in section 4.3. Moreover there is the KPI "Activity Duration" defined and calculated by the CEP Engine. Also there are activity-instance indicators (indicatorlevel_id = 3) and process indicators defined (= 1). The process level thereby has average and percentage indicators. Moreover there are KPIs (indicator_type id = 2), environmental indicators (= 4) and KEIs (= 1) defined.

This table is needed for the "indicator" table, which does include the "indicatordefinition_id" as a foreign key, a correlation id and the calculated indicator value. The issue with this correlation id was already mentioned before, as it could be the primary key of a process, process-instance, activity or activity-instance. It results in the necessity to identify which entity (process, process-instance, etc.) the correlation ID belongs to. That is the reason why the database creates a new ID for activities and processes. Because of this correlation ID and the "indicator level" table connected by the "indicator definition" table it is possible to determine the corresponding entity of an indicator and enables to persist all classes of indicators in one table. This is why the table "indicator" is connected to one or zero process, process-instance, activity or activity-instance and will be identified by the indicator definition table, which includes the indicator level. Thus actually level is determined by indicator level plus correlation id. With this basis it is possible to store different kinds of indicators on all possible abstraction levels and provides the best flexibility for this framework.

Finally the definition of KEIs specified target values that must be set to define a desired situation. It would indicate the difference between nominal and actual business situation. A means is needed to defined targets for indicators on different abstraction levels. The first design did add a simple target value field to the indicator table. But there are also indicators on activity-instance level, which usually don't have target values assigned. This would lead to a huge amount of null values, as there are many entries on activity-instance level. So another approach has been realized that separates target values from the actual calculated values. It uses a table "indicator target" that includes the "indicatordefinition id", "indicatorlevel id" and "correlation id" as foreign keys and a target value. It is illustrated in Figure 29 and contains the target values ESOR has set to their KEIs. They have been identified after some process-instances were executed and the indicators have been calculated. Except for the percentage of renewable electricity for which the target value was set to 80 percent.

This approach provides the ability to define target values for each indicator level and indicator definition for a process, activity, etc. and is connected to all these tables.

target_id	indicatordefinition_id	indicatorlevel_id	correlation_id	target_value
1	10	1	1	0.800000
2	8	1	1	5.000000
3	6	1	1	0.500000
4	7	1	1	0.001000
5	9	1	1	0.000400

Figure 29 - Table Indicator Target

With this Datawarehouse design the KEI framework provides a very flexible structure to persist all monitored data. These are used to calculate different classes of KEIs and other indicators defined in the "indicator definition" table. It is possible to persist the calculated KEIs in the DW. Moreover it is feasible to set target values, so is possible to visualize KEIs.

4.4.5 Extract Transform Load Process

To insert the monitored data into the DW, a method is needed that inserts these data into the Datawarehouse and transforms the electricity consumption that was simulated to emission of carbon dioxide and atomic waste and electricity costs. A so-called Extract Transform Load process usually provides such functionalities. Resulting in the fact that some kind of "buffer" is needed that stores the monitored data until this ETL process is executed. This buffer is often realized as a database, which is usually called an "Operational Data Store" (ODS). It contains all events and information that occurred until the ETL process will be executed This will fill the Datawarehouse. Often it is started during the night, when nobody is working therewith resources are not overloaded and used when not needed.

These statements result actually in two design choices that have to be made. First how the "buffer" is realized and second when and how often this ETL process is going to be invoked. These choices depend especially on the time and profitability aspects of the economical requirement that was set for KEIs. Unfortunately it is not known which aspects are more relevant for ESOR, profitability or time so it will be assumed that ESOR has the focus on profitability rather than time. Moreover depending on the ambition of the later analysis another design could result. This case study assumes that data on a daily basis is sufficient. Starting with the discussion how the ODS will be realized. ESOR has already a messaging structure available in their existing systems by using Apache ActiveMQ. So this "buffer" could also be realized by using messaging services. Thus three different implementing opportunities for realizing the ODS are:

- Database
- Point-to-Point (Queue)
    - Polling Consumer
    - Event-driven Consumer
- Publish-Subscribe (Topic)

For this case study it was decided to use the messaging infrastructure for realizing the buffer instead of a database approach, as it is already available and does not have any disadvantages to databases. Nevertheless there are still two choices to make. One should think about the necessity to send messages to more destinations, which would imply to use a publish-subscribe approach with the ETL process. The ETL process should be a durable subscriber as all monitoring messages are needed to ensure consistency of the Datawarehouse and using a normal subscription would lead to missing data as they are only published once. If the ETL process would be down it would miss messages. But as ESOR does not have in mind to build other systems that are interested in this monitoring data, a point-to-point channel is satisfying by using a queue as buffer until the ETL process is executed. Even if this information is needed by another system it could extract it from the Datawarehouse or a second queue could be defined to which the "EventManager" sends its events, too. After deciding to use a Queue as the buffer the ETL process could be a polling or event-driven consumer. A polling consumer would actively request messages from the Queue if it wants to consume messages. A message listener would inform an event-driven consumer that new messages arrived. Separating these two possibilities an event-driven consumer would be more useful if a Queue is empty for an extended period of time. On the other hand a polling-consumer could be started and will request for messages until it is stopped again. This is the approach that is implemented for the ETL process, as ESOR plans to execute the ETL process during the night so that the queue does contain a lot of messages when starting the ETL process. The event-driven consumer would make no sense. Even if they want to fill the Datawarehouse in real time the polling consumer could always run, but if there were times when no messages are in the Queue this would be not sufficient.

A requirement was to persist the indicators calculated by the CEP engine the ETL process was actually divided into two parts. It first gets all events from the "ODS Queue" which is the buffer that the "EventManager" sends its events to with the simulated environmental data, inserts all data to the Datawarehouse and afterwards gets all events from the "CEP Queue" used by the CEP engine to send its measured indicator "activity duration" to. These two routines are tried to illustrate in Figure 31 as a sequence diagram where there are two loops, the first one for the ODS Queue and the second for the CEP Queue. Therefore the CEP Engine was expanded to send messages to the "CEP Queue". It creates a "CEPEvent" (illustrated in Figure 30) with the measured data, and sends it to the CEP Queue used by ETL.

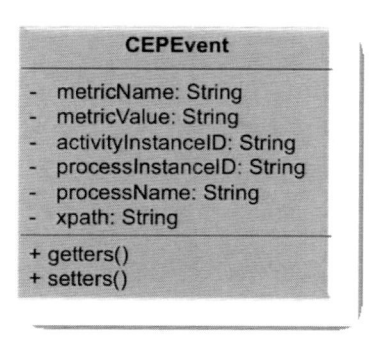

```
              CEPEvent
  - metricName: String
  - metricValue: String
  - activityInstanceID: String
  - processInstanceID: String
  - processName: String
  - xpath: String
  + getters()
  + setters()
```

Figure 30 - Class diagram CEP Event

Firstly, it is explained how the ETL process for the ODS Queue is executed. It is divided into three monitoring routines, one for process, process-instance and activity-instance events. If it is a process event, it will be checked whether it is already contained in the Datawarehouse. If not almost all data can be simply read from the event for insertion. A certain issue evolved to insert the BPEL file into the Datawarehouse as Apache ODE. This does only provide the path to the BPEL file so that it was necessary to include a file reader to get the content of it and transform special characters, like quotes, to a string-conform sequence of characters. After this was done the data could be simply inserted into the Datawarehouse. The "process_id" will be auto-generated by the database and not calculated by this routine itself, so the insert statement contains a null value for this attribute. If it gets a message that is a process-instance event the data can also be simply read from the corresponding event, but as the time and date table were separated a further routine is needed. Therefore two calendar values are created based on two timestamps one is read from the start event and one from the end event that are contained in the process-instance event.

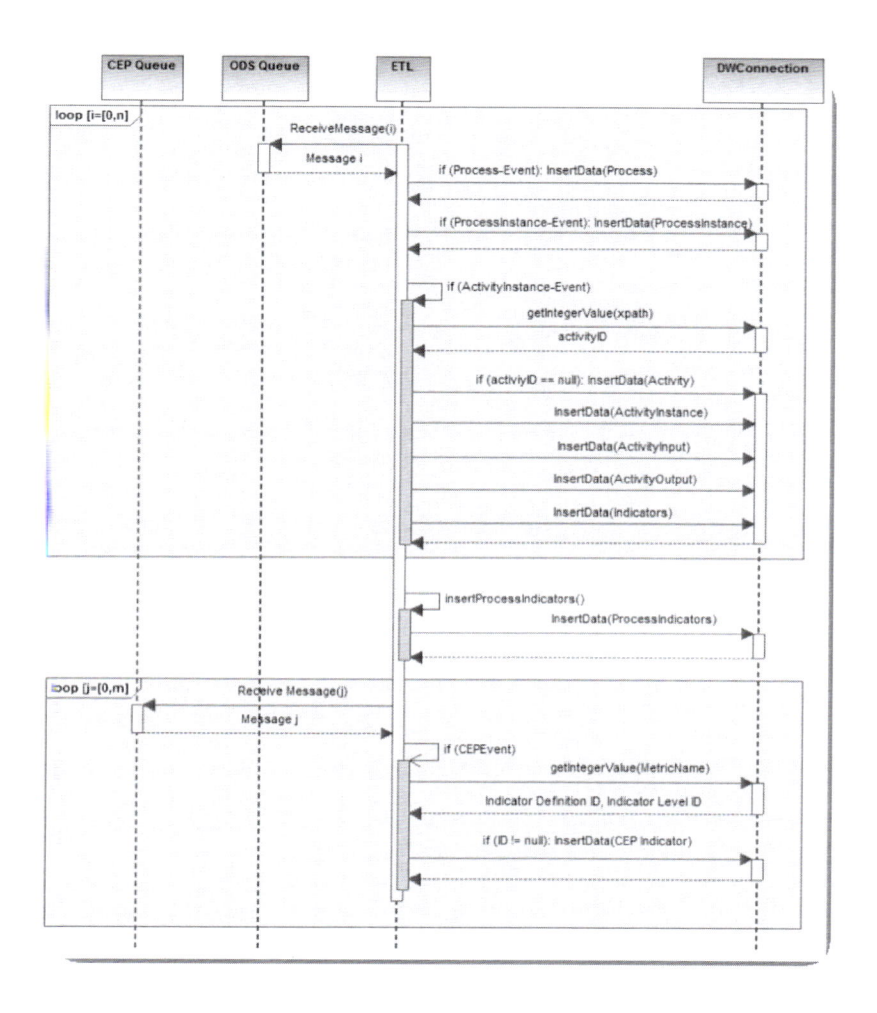

Figure 31 - Sequence Diagram ETL Process

To insert the date and time entries and connect them to process-instance events, a procedure is needed that returns the primary key produced by the database when the time and date entries are inserted into the Datawarehouse. So there is a routine that gets a GregorianCalendar Instance based on the time stamp to check if a entry for this specific date and time does exists and if not inserts it. The "insert date" routine does contain a hard coded standard definition of a quarter. It could be outsourced to a database so that a corporation can define it. Finally it returns the corresponding id to set it for the process-instance event as foreign key to add time and date dependency. Afterwards it will be inserted into the Datawarehouse. The process-instance ETL routine is actually not illustrated in the figure for a better overview.

Finally it comes to activity-instance events. These are more complicated, as it contains several aspects. It inserts the activity-instance and activity, the caused input and output of the activity and finally inserts the indicators that are defined on activity-instance basis. To insert an activity-instance, the required data are extracted from the activity-instance event and also the date and time dependencies are calculated in the same way as for process-instances. As there are no activity events the procedure checks if an activity with the xpath contained in the activity-instance event does exist. If not it creates a new activity entry to the Datawarehouse, through that the issue is solved. Next it calculates the used inputs, which is only electricity in this case and inserts this information into the activity-instance input table. The activity-instance output routine transforms this input to the caused emission of carbon dioxide and atomic waste by using the energy-mix table for transformation. As an external activity uses electricity within the execution engine of ESOR and has a SLA annotated both carbon dioxide emission are added. After these transformations they are inserted into the Datawarehouse.

The last step for activity-instance events is the insertion of the defined indicators for them. So it contains a procedure that contains the methods used to calculate or simply get these indicators from the corresponding input and output of the activity-instance, like caused atomic waste or used electricity on activity-instance basis. It also inserts them into the indicator table, so that inputs and outputs are separated from the facts of interest that are represented as an indicator. In this case these activity-indicators are solely extracted and almost no aggregation is done except by adding carbon dioxide emission from used electricity for executing the activity in Apache ODE and carbon dioxide caused by the external partner. Nevertheless this routine is useful if artificial-based indicators are going to be calculated so that different substances are aggregated. The procedure "calculation of process indicators" will be shown in the next section as it contains aggregation routines.

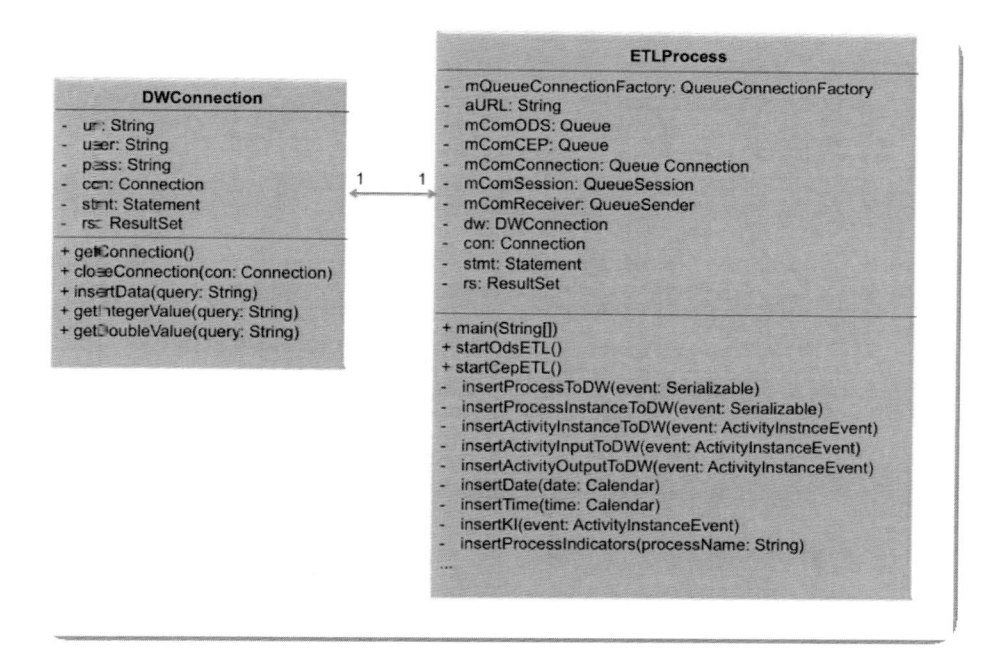

Figure 32 - Class diagram - ETL and DWConnection

The CEP insertion procedure raised a certain issue, as indicators can be calculated on different levels, as activity-instances, process-instances and processes. Using the indicator definition table solved this issue. The ETL process actually is querying this table based on the "metricName" included in the CEPEvent. If an "indicatordefinition" that includes information about the "indicator level" is available in the Datawarehouse the data will be inserted into the "indicator" table. The correlation ID is set depending on the identified level, so if the indicator definition is on activity-instance level, the activityInstanceID will be used.

Finally a class diagram of the ETL process and the connected "DWConnection" class is illustrated in Figure 32. The ETL uses the "DWConnection" to connect to the Datawarehouse and insert Queries as well as read single data by its provided methods. If a dataset should be read the ETL does execute this query itself, as a "DataSet" is not returnable by a method. Moreover the ETL class does contain several methods used to separate the different insertion routines, whereby the ones used to calculate indicators are not visualized for a better overview.

4.4.6 Aggregation of data and calculation of KEIs

After it has been shown how the ETL process is executed it comes to the aggregation and calculation of KEIs done by the component "decision support system". As was said in section 4.4.4, indicators can be calculated on every level such as process, process-instance, activity and activity-instance.

Thus two approaches are thinkable. One could aggregate data and calculate KEIs every time the dashboard makes a request. An example for such an aggregation on activity level is shown in the next section. It results in real-time data if the ETL process is always running. The other option would be to include aggregation and calculation logic into the ETL process so that indicators and KEIs are already calculated if a dashboard requested them. This approach does only make sense if executing the ETL process for example once a day. This is implemented in this way.

Figure 31 already includes three methods that are used to calculate or insert indicators by the ETL process. One of them is the ETL routine for "CEPEvents" that simply inserts the calculated metric into the DW. Two methods of the ODS ETL routine are used for calculating ESORs KEIs. If activity-instances are inserted into the Datawarehouse the identified KEIs of ESOR are already inserted on activity-instance basis by the "Insert Key Indicators" arrow. In this case it is actually not a calculation but an extract of the input and outputs of the activity-instance. Solely the gathered electricity consumption, CO_2 emission, etc. are written into the indicators table as it was defined as a KEI. As no target values are set on activity-instance level it would not be possible to visualize these KEIs. This would also not follow its definition. Moreover it is questionable if objectives made to a process will be specified to individual activity-instances. Even though they are categorized as KEIs in the Datawarehouse they cannot be used for visualization of KEIs.

It results in the necessity to aggregate them to higher levels. This is enabled by the "insertProcessIndicators()" method of the ETL process that is invoked after all messages contained in the ODS Queue are inserted. Thereby a method for calculating each KEI on process-level, selected in section 4.3 is implemented, as well as further ones for calculating absolute atomic waste for instance. For a better flexibility the "insertProcessIndicators()" method does read a xml, which defines indicators to be calculated for a specific process name.

It could define that for ESORs ordering process absolute electricity consumption should be calculated. The "insertProcessIndicators()" method would invoke the calculation method "absoluteElectricityConsumption()" that defines how this indicator is calculated and inserted into the DW. As a result, indicators that are going to be calculated can be defined for each process individually.

For each identified KEI and indicator for ESOR, a corresponding method is implemented to aggregate and calculate it. Finally it will insert it into the DW or update it in case it was already calculated once.

As a KEI is representing a current business situation a certain issue evolves. This has been discussed in section 3.1. It had been identified that "current" means a certain period of time into the past indicating the current situation defined individually for each corporation. As ESOR wants to optimize its ordering-process the current situation is understood as since the last process change, represented by the process name. The implemented calculation methods assume that calculating KEIs is done by aggregation of all activity-instance connected to it, caused by the fact that the process name changes if the business-process would do. The process name is used to indicate the current situation and not the date- and time- tables.

Finally an example will be shown for calculating the KEI "average Electricity Consumption". The corresponding method implemented in the ETL process named "averageElectricityConsumption()" provides this calculation. First it is aggregating all electricity usage indicators stored in the indicator table by summing up the individual values of electricity consumption connected to its activity-instances getting the absolute amount of electricity used for this process and divides this value by the amount of its corresponding process-instances that have been executed. This value will be inserted into the indicator table of the Datawarehouse or updated depending whether this indicator for this process was calculated before and solely updates the value to the current state.

4.4.7 Visualization of KEIs

Finally it comes to step three of Figure 1 "deploy management dashboard system". That is also used for the "decision support module" of environmental accounting and the "analysis" phase of the BPM lifecycle, which can now be done on the basis of environmental objectives.

It is assumed that the dashboard is created for the process-owner. To provide him with relevant information one should think about which information he could need. In regard to optimize environmental impact of his process by the BPM lifecycle, he first wants to get a general overview illustrating the actual process situation and its difference to the specified targets. Next he wants to see all indicators that are calculated for this single process, as well as get information about which activities are causing the most environmental impact. Finally he could be interested in the BPEL File, as it enables a more detailed analysis.

Next it is considered is in which way are the gathered data or indicators presented. A classical local Graphical User Interface (GUI) or a Web User Interface (WUI) could be used to present information for decision support. As Web Applications are more flexible concerning access to this information, plus tablets and smartphones are becoming more and more popular, ESOR decided to implement a Management Dashboard for KEIs as a WUI. Moreover it has been implemented by Java Server Pages that enable to use Java Code for connection to the Datawarehouse and implementing the dashboard logic. The concrete style of this dashboard is outsourced into a Cascading Style Sheet File to completely separate design from the content. For building the charts and table the Google Chart Application Programming Interface (API) was used. It provides a simple way to create charts. Actually it is a java script and can be fed with the data from the Datawarehouse.

To visualize indicators there are many possibilities available. They could be represented in a spreadsheet with certain information like date or division included. Further the process of calculation could be visualized with concrete data. Another possibility is to visualize them in a cockpit including graphs, diagrams or other graphical representations.[138] In this case study they will be visualized in a dashboard based on the previous introduced Datawarehouse-schema. The basis for this visualization is the simulation of data that is going to be extracted into the Datawarehouse and the calculation of different kinds of indicators. Moreover a target value is needed to visualize KEIs as the definition specified. So the chosen visualization must be able to include two values: the actual and the target value. The easiest opportunity to visualize this is a spreadsheet, containing the indicators name, type, value and target value. These could actually visualize KEIs. This approach is chosen for the process page and it illustrates all indicators defined in the indicators table of the Datawarehouse that are correlated to a certain process and does have a target value if one was set.

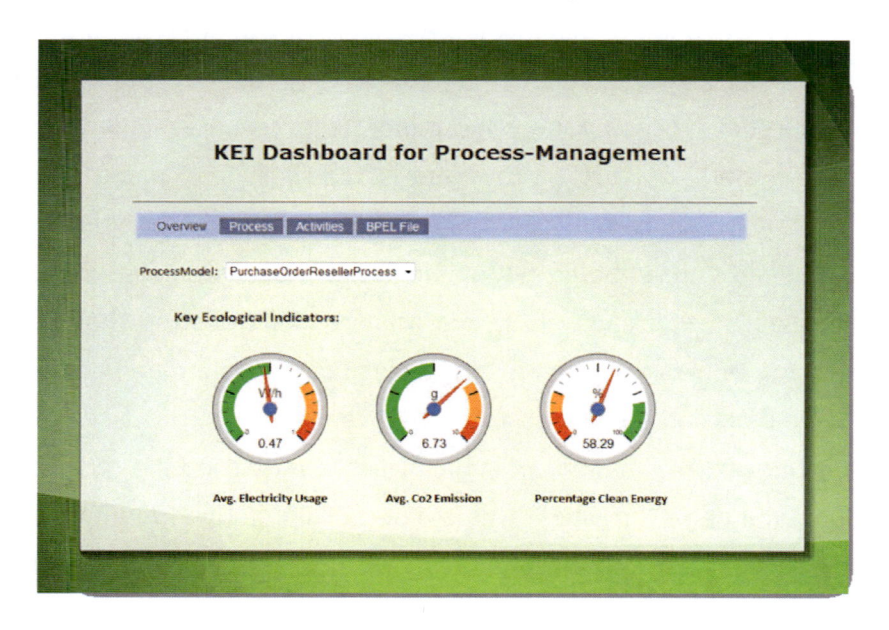

Figure 33 - Dashboard for ESOR – Overview

---

[138] Cf. Pollmann, R., Rühm, P. (2007), p.65.

For visualizing KEIs some kind of graphical representation would be helpful to get a good overview. This graphical representation should be able to represent the tuple a KEI consists of. The chosen "speedometer" represents a subset of ESORs KEIs and is illustrated in Figure 33. It indicates the current business-process situation by the pin and the target value set by highlighting the corresponding area in which the target is reached green. The red and yellow areas are calculated by multiplying the target value by two. The red area actually is set from ninety to hundred percent of the doubled target value. The yellow area is defined from seventy to ninety percent of it. It illustrates whether a KEI is differing too much from the target value.

It should be mentioned that setting targets for the identified absolute KEIs, like total electricity consumption, is only possible if the current situation is specified as a constant period of time (a year for instance). If done so it shows progress in reducing the processes' total impact. The period of time is varying in the current business situation, which is represented in this case study by the actual process version. Because of this fact it makes it nearly impossible to define target values for them. Regarding this statement they are not visualized in the overview, but in the process page without any target value assigned. Nonetheless they are stated as KEIs as they are strategically connected to ESORs strategy, but cannot be used for optimizing a business-process in this case. The only aspects usable for strategically optimize the process concerning its environmental impact in this case study are relative indicators, so that the three KEIs percentage of clean energy, average electricity consumption and average carbon dioxide emission are visualized in the overview.

Moreover to provide information, which activities are causing the most environmental impact the page "activities" was created (illustrated in Figure 34). Its aggregation is done every time the dashboard does make a query. It aggregates activity-instance indicators to activity-level and illustrates each activity with its relative impact to the processes electricity consumption. This is represented by a pie chart. It makes it possible to prioritize demand for actions concerning concrete activities of a process. For each page there is a select box for choosing a certain process and makes it possible to illustrate different processes and their contribution in following a strategy. Furthermore it enables to see progress of optimizations by selecting the old and new version of a process indicated by process name.

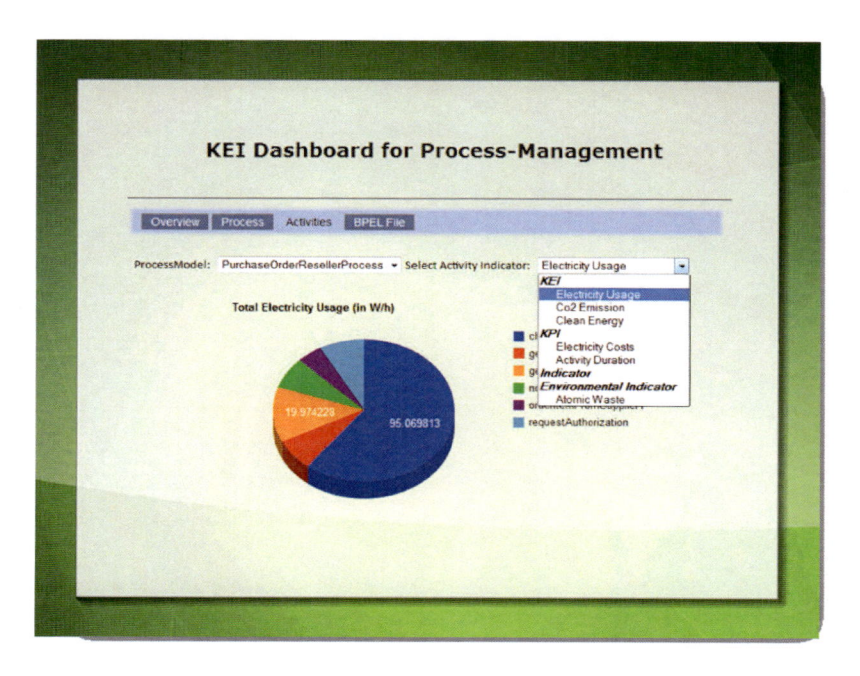

Figure 34 – Dashboard for ESOR – Activities

With the establishment of the decision support system, the purpose of this work to identify and visualize KEIs has been fulfilled and the BPM lifecycle has been extended by environmental data enabled by the modules of environmental-accounting.

It is the basis to execute the next steps: identify potentials to optimize environmental impact of business-processes strategically and control performance.

5. Conclusion

In the introduction different motivations for enterprises have been shown to reduce their environmental impact. To manage the present environmental impact the saying "if you measure it, you can manage it" has been given a hint how to operationalize this endeavor.

Before discussing the concept of KEIs on a theoretical basis some environmental foundations have been necessary. Therefore sustainability has been discussed, as it has been helpful to identify an environmental strategy for the case study. The perspective on ecology has been shown its relevance and illustrated different understandings concerning ecology.

Afterwards the functions of the nature: "provisioning", "regulating", "supporting services" and "cultural and an amenity" have been shown. As a result the economic sector and especially its processes primarily rely on provisioning and regulating functions provided by our ecological system.

On this basis the health of nature has been discussed, and how this could be one strategically goal of corporations. Therefore health of nature is given if sustainable development of nature is ensured. Further it has been shown that the understanding of environmental health from corporations is often limited. Nevertheless conditions of environmental health have been illustrated for corporations seeing environmental health as strategically relevant.

After the environmental basics have been established, the definition of KEIs has been derived out of the definition of indicators, KPIs and environmental indicators. Additionally several issues concerning terminologies have been discussed. As a result KEIs were understood as an indication of a particular, actual business situation and its environmental impact. They are tied to strategic targets concerning ecology by setting target values. The issue to identify what "current" business situation means has also been discussed, as it has been relevant for the calculation of KEIs in the practical part of this work. In regard to visualize KEIs they have been further defined as a tuple consisting of ecological characteristics metric and a target value function.

Also looking at requirements for indicators has identified different requirements to KEIs. It resulted that KEIs should fulfill the requirements economical requirement, relevancy, measurability, environmental reference and transparency. Those had an influence on several design decisions for the KEI framework.

To differentiate diverse kinds of KEIs they have been classified by the level of detail (corporation, processes, products), whereby processes were further specified (process, process-instance, activity, activity-instance). Afterwards KEIs are classified based on their scale of unit (resources-based, monetary-based, artificial-based).

Afterwards the macro-view was illustrated for getting a better context and relation to the micro-view. The micro-view has been understood as the environmental impact of a corporation. Therefore the concept of environmental management was introduced and compared to the BPM lifecycle to identify how it could be expanded by environmental information. As a result the concept of environmental-accounting has been illustrated that it is usable for identifying and visualizing KEIs. It has led to the solution to expand "monitoring" and "analysis" phases of the BPM lifecycle by modules needed for environmental-accounting.

Based on this knowledge it has been shown that KEIs could be determined in a top-down or bottom-up approach. It contained to gather the actual environmental impact and a strategy that is represented by target values for monitoring progress in reaching this strategy. Moreover a mutual dependence has been shown. In regard for calculating KEIs a substances and energy flux analysis has been identified to be a very flexible approach. After the process to identify KEIs has been shown, several resource-, monetary and artificial-based environmental indicators have been illustrated that might be KEIs depending on whether they are connected to strategy. At last some basic principles have been shown to ensure sustainable development to give hints for possible strategies concerning environmental impact.

After these theoretical basics the building of a KEI framework for business-processes has been shown. This was done on a case study for one business-process. By specifying the context of the case study and different properties to the framework the module "ambition" of environmental-accounting was executed. It resulted in the KEIs that were identified for ESOR.

Next the "information system" module of environmental accounting was integrated to the "monitoring" phase of the BPM lifecycle. It has been shown how ESOR can measure environmental impact on activity-instance level by the "EventManager" and "Eco Simulator" components.

Furthermore a Datawarehouse has been designed that is needed for both modules "information system" and "decision support system" of environmental accounting and the "monitoring" and "analysis" phases of the BPM lifecycle. It enabled to store monitored data about processes, their environmental impacts and the calculated indicators.

The functioning of the ETL process has been shown and was used to insert monitored data into the DW and make transformations needed to calculate emission of purchased stuff or the amount of clean energy used. Moreover it contained methods that calculate KEIs and other indicators during its execution.

Finally this data was used to build a decision support system in terms of a management-dashboard and has been the basis for "analysis" phase of the BPM lifecycle. The calculated KEIs were presented in an overview and the impacts of the activities were illustrated in a pie chart, so that demand for action can be identified. With this information the business-process could be optimized by its environmental impact in a strategically way.

In conclusion a flexible KEI framework for business-processes has been created that implemented the identified components required for environmental-accounting. It enabled to execute the BPM lifecycle with regard to decrease environmental performance. Therefore it expanded its monitoring and analysis phases with KEIs. As a result this KEI framework is enabling corporations to reduce environmental impact of their business-processes in a strategically oriented manner.

6. Outlook

Finally a brief outlook on this topic will be given. Environmental problems like the greenhouse effect are getting visible. As governments can influence contributions of its nation and economy it is a very important possibility to coordinate actions made to environmental protection. It results that the link between macro- and micro-view should be examined more extensively, so that governments can set regulations that ensure sustainable development. Maybe even the illustrated absolute authority would be created to ensure environmental health.

In the micro-view new KEIs might be invented expressing environmental impact realistically in one single indicator that can be visualized and compresses more information. Or a set of KEIs might be developed that are usable for all corporations so that a general Framework can be build which t is usable to all corporations.

Maybe even KEIs can be visualized in a better way. For example SAP bought a corporation specialized in visualizing business data (like information about products or processes) in 3D.[139] This indicates that SAP is seeing a potential in such a three dimensional visualization approach. It is questionable if such visualization approach would actually offer added value. Nevertheless it might be sufficient for some cases.

---

[139] Golem (2011), URL see references

7. References

Books:

Braun, B. (2002) Unternehmen zwischen ökologischen und ökonomischen Zielen – Konzepte, Akteure und Chancen des industriellen Umweltmanagements aus wirtschaftsgeographischer Sicht, 1. Auflage, Münster 2002

Bryman, A., Cramer, D. (2009) Constructing Variables, p.17-34, In: Bryman, A., Hardy, M. A. The Handbook of Data Analysis, Paperback Edition, London 2009

Burkert, M. (2008) Qualität von Kennzahlen und Erfolg von Managern – Direkte, indirekte und moderierende Effekte, 1. Auflage, Wiesbaden 2008

Buß, E. (2007) Die deutschen Spitzenmanager – Wie sie wurden, was sie sind – Herkunft, Wertvorstellungen, Erfolgsregeln, First Edition, München 2007

Buß, E. (2009) Managementsoziologie – Grundlagen, Praxiskonzepte, Fallstudien, 2., korrigierte Auflage, München 2009

Clausen, J. (1998) Umweltkennzahlen als Steuerungsinstrument für das nachhaltige Wirtschaften von Unternehmen, p.33-70, in: Seidel, E., Clausen, J., Seifert, E.K., Umweltkennzahlen – Planungs-, Steuerungs- und Kontrollgrößen für ein umweltorientiertes Management, First Edition, München 1998

Conner, N. (2009) Living Green: The Missing Manual, First Edition, Sebastopol 2009

DeSimone, L. D., Popoff, F., World Business Council for Sustainable Development (1997) Eco-Efficiency – The Business Link to Sustainable Development, First Edition, Massachusetts 1997

Dietrich, E., Schulze, A., Weber, S. (2007) Kennzahlensystem für die Qualitätsbeurteilung in der industriellen Produktion, 1. Auflage, München 2007

Dietz, S., Neumayer, E. (2006) A critical appraisal of genuine savings as an indicator of sustainability, p.117-138, in: Lawn, P. (2006) Sustainable Development Indicators in Ecological Economics, First Edition, Massachusetts 2006

Faßenbender-Wynands, E., Seuring, S.A. (2001) Grundlagen des Umweltcontrolling – Aufgaben, Instrumente, Organisation, p.139-153, in: Baumast, A., Pape, J. (Hrsg.) - Betriebliches Umweltmanagement - Theoretische Grundlagen; Praxisbeispiele, 1. Auflage, Stuttgart 2001

Feller, M., Göllinger, T., Weber, F.M. (1998) Umweltkennzahlen im Handel, p.215-246, in: Seidel, E., Clausen, J., Seifert, E.K. - Umweltkennzahlen – Planungs-, Steuerungs- und Kontrollgrößen für ein umweltorientiertes Management, First Edition, München 1998

Friedman, F.B. (2003) Practical Guide to Environmental Management, 9th Edition, Washington 2003

Gladen, W. (2008) Performance Measurement – Controlling mit Kennzahlen, 4. überarbeitete Auflage, Wiesbaden 2008

Groot, R., Hein, L., Kroeze, C., Leemans, R. Niemeijer, D. (2006) Indicators and measures of critical natural capital, p.221-245, in: Lawn, P. (2006) Sustainable Development Indicators in Ecological Economics, First Edition, Massachusetts 2006

Große, H., Ehrig, S., Lehmann, G. (2000) Umweltschutz und Umweltmanagement in der gewerblichen Wirtschaft – EMAS und ISO 14001 in Praxis und Entwicklung – ein Leitfaden, First Edition, Renningen 2000

Grubb, M., Vrolijk, C., Brack, D. (1999) The Kyoto Protocol – A Guide and Assessment, First Edition, Washington 1999

Gruber, K.A. (2009) Der Begriff der gesellschaftlichen Verantwortung und seine Ausgestaltung durch Unternehmen – Eine Illustration am Beispiel der deutschen Automobilhersteller, 1. Auflage, Marburg 2009

Grunwald, A., Kopfmüller, J. (2006) Nachhaltigkeit, 1. Auflage, Frankfurt 2006

Harmsen, J., Powell, J.B. (2010) Sustainable Development in the Process Industries – Cases and Impact, First Edition, Hoboken 2010

Heuer, A., Saake, G., Sattler, K.U. (2008) Datenbanken – Konzepte und Sprachen, 3. aktualisierte und erweiterte Auflage, Heidelberg 2008

Hilgenkamp, K. (2006) Environmental Health – Ecological Perspectives, First Edition, Sudbury 2006

Hopfenbeck, W., Jasch, C., Jasch, A. (1996) Lexikon des Umweltmanagements, First edition, Landsberg 1996

Hüttner, K.-L. (2001) Inhaltliche und konzeptionelle Einordnung von Nachhaltigkeitsindikatoren des SFB 525, p.43-63, in: Kuckshinrich, W., Hüttner, K.-L. (Hrsg.), Nachhaltiges Management metallischer Stoffströme: Indikatoren und deren Anwendung, Kerkrade 2001

Inmon, W.H. (2005) Building the Data Warehouse, Fourth Edition, Indianapolis 2005

Jorgensen, S.E. (2010), Introduction, p.3-8, in: Jorgensen, S.E., Xu, F.L., Costanza, R. - Handbook of Ecological Indicators for Assessment of Ecosystem Health, Second Edition, Boca Raton 2010

Jorgensen, S.E., Xu., F.L., Marques, C., Salas, F. (2010), Application of Indicators for the Assessment of Ecosystem Health, p.9-46, in: Jorgensen, S.E., Xu, F.L., Costanza, R. - Handbook of Ecological Indicators for Assessment of Ecosystem Health, Second Edition, Boca Raton 2010

Kamiske, G.F., Butterbrodt, D., Dannich-Kappelmann, M., Tammler, U. (1995) Umweltmanagement: Moderne Methoden und Techniken zur Umsetzung, First Edition, München/Wien 1995

Kanning, H., Müller, M. (2001) Bedeutung des Nachhaltigkeitsbildes (sustainable development) für das betriebliche Managament, p.13-27, in: Baumast, A., Pape, J. (Hrsg.) - Betriebliches Umweltmanagement - Theoretische Grundlagen; Praxisbeispiele, 1. Auflage, Stuttgart 2001

Kesselmann, M. Krieger, J. (2009) Introduction, p.1-34, in: Kesselmann, M., Krieger, J., - European Politics in Transition, 6th Edition, Boston 2009

Kottmann, H., Loew, T., Clausen, J. (1999) Umweltmanagement mit Kennzahlen, First Edition, München 1999

Kress, M. (2010) Intelligent Business Process Optimization for the Service Industry, Karlsruhe 2010

Küker, S. (2003) Kooperation und Nachhaltigkeit: ein prozessorientierter Gestaltungsansatz für eine Analyse der Beiträge von Koope- rationen zum nachhaltigen Wirtschaften, Hamburg 2003

Lawn, P. (2006) Sustainable development: concept and indicators, p.13-54, in: Lawn, P. (2006) Sustainable Development Indicators in Ecological Economics, First Edition, Massachusetts 2006

Lesourd, J.B., Schilizzi, S.G.M. (2001) The Environment in Corporate Management – New Directions and Economic Insights, First Edition, Massachusetts 2001

Lintott, J. (2006) Environmental accounting and policy making, p.78-95, in: Lawn, P. (2006) Sustainable Development Indicators in Ecological Economics, First Edition, Massachusetts 2006

Milon, J.W., Shogren, J.F. (1995) Integrating Economic and Ecological Indicators – Practical Methods for Environmental Policy Analysis, First Edition, Westport 1995

Müller, A. (2010) Umweltorientiertes betriebliches Rechnungswesen, 3. Vollständig überarbeitete und erweiterte Auflage, München 2010

Niccolucci, V., Pulselli, R.M., Focardi, S. Bastianoni, S. (2010), Integrated Indicators for Evaluating Ecosystem Health, p.425-446, in: Jorgensen, S.E., Xu, F.L., Costanza, R. - Handbook of Ecological Indicators for Assessment of Ecosystem Health, Second Edition, Boca Raton 2010

Nowak, A., Leymann, F., Mietzner, R. (2010) Towards Green Business Process Reengineering. In: Proceedings of the First International Workshop on Services, Energy, & Ecosystem: SEE2010, pp. 187-1952. San Francisco, USA, December 07, 2010.

Nowak, A., Leymann, F., Schumm, D., Wetzstein, B. (2011) An Architecture and Methodology for a Four-Phased Approach to Green Business Process Geengineering, p.150-164, in: Proceedings of the 1. International Conference on ICT as Key Technology for the Fight against Global Warming

Oberthür, S., Ott, H.E. (1999) The Kyoto Protocol – International Climate Policy for the 21st Century, First Edition, Berlin/Heidelberg 1999

Olson, E.G. (2009) Better Green Business – Handbook for environmentally responsible and profitable business practices, First Edition, New Jersey 2009

Ösze, D. (2000) Managementinformationen im New Public Management – am Beispiel der Steuerverwaltung des Kantons Bern, Wien 2000

Pape, J., Pick, E., Goebels, T. (2001) Umweltkennzahlen und –systeme zur Umweltleistungsbewertung, p.178-192, in: Baumast, A., Pape, J. (Hrsg.) - Betriebliches Umweltmanagement - Theoretische Grundlagen; Praxisbeispiele, 1. Auflage, Stuttgart 2001

Parisi, C., Maraghini, M.P. (2010) Operationalising Sustainability: How Small and Medium Sized Enterprises Translate Social and Environmental Issues into Practice, p.131-148, in: Taticchi, P. (Hrsg.) - Business Performance Measurement and Management), First Edition, Perugia 2010

Parmenter, D. (2010) Key Performance Indicators – Developing, Implementing and Using Winning KPIs, Second Edition, New Jersey 2010

Pollmann, R., Rühm, P. (2007) Controlling-Berichte professionell gestalten, 1. Auflage, München 2007

Rasmussen, N., Chen, C.Y., Bansal, M. (2009) Business Dashboards – A Visual Catalog for Design and Deployment, First Edition, New Jersey 2009

Roberts, J. (2011) Environmental Policy, Second Edition, Abingdon 2011

Schaltegger, S., Dylilick, T. (2002) Nachhaltig managen mit der Balanced Scorecard, Wiesbaden 2002

Schaltegger, S., Sturm, A. (1995) Öko-Effizienz durch Öko-Controlling – Zur praktischen Umsetzung von EMAS und ISO 14001, First Edition, Stuttgart 1995

Seidel, E., (1998) Umweltorientierte Kennzahlen und Kennzahlensysteme – Leistungsmöglichkeiten und Leistungsgrenzen, Entwicklungsstand und Entwicklungsaussichten, p.9-32, in: Seidel, E., Clausen, J., Seifert, E.K. - Umweltkennzahlen – Planungs-, Steuerungs- und Kontrollgrößen für ein umweltorientiertes Management, First Edition, München 1998

Seidel, E., Koch, C., Stahlschmidt A. (1998a) Umweltkennzahlen in Banken, p.175-214, in: Seidel, E., Clausen, J., Seifert, E.K. - Umweltkennzahlen – Planungs-, Steuerungs- und Kontrollgrößen für ein umweltorientiertes Management, First Edition, München 1998

Seidel, E., Lossie, A., Weber, F.M. (1998b) Umweltkennzahlen in der Industrie, p.141-174, in: Seidel, E., Clausen, J., Seifert, E.K. - Umweltkennzahlen – Planungs-, Steuerungs- und Kontrollgrößen für ein umweltorientiertes Management, First Edition, München 1998

Senge, P., Smith, B., Kruschwitz, N., Laur, J., Schley, S. (2008) The Necessary Revolution – How Individuals and Organisations are Working Together to Create a Sustainable World, First Edition, London 2008

Seurig, S.A., Pick, E. (2001) Stoff- und Energieflussanalysen, p.154-164, in: Baumast, A., Pape, J. (Hrsg.) - Betriebliches Umweltmanagement - Theoretische Grundlagen; Praxisbeispiele, 1. Auflage, Stuttgart 2001

Shakhaschiri, B.Z. (1989) Chemical Demonstrations – A Handbook for Teachers of Chemistry - Volume 3, First Edition, Wisconsin 1989

Sheldon, C., Yoxon, M. (2002) Installing Environmental Management System – A Step-By-Step Guide, Revised Edition, London 2002

Wackernagel, M., Moran, D. White, S., Murray, M. (2006) Ecological Foortpring accounts for advancing sustainability: measuring human demands on nature, p.246-267, in: Lawn, P. (2006) Sustainable Development Indicators in Ecological Economics, First Edition, Massachusetts 2006

Wackernagel, M., Rees, W. (1996) Our Ecological Footprint – Reducing Human Impact on the Earth, First Edition, Gabriola Island 1996

Wilkens, S. (2007) Effizientes Nachhaltigkeitsmanagement, Wiesbaden 2007

Windsor, S. (2010) An Introduction to Green Process Management, First Edition, Milwaukee 2010

Zee, H. (2002) Measuring the Value of Information Technology, First Edition, Hershey 2002

Papers:

Eichhorn, P. (1976) Gesellschaftsbezogene Unternehmensrechnung und betriebswirtschaftliche Sozialindikatoren, in: ZfbF-Sonderheft, 5/1976, S.159-169

Priyantha, N.B., Kansal, A., Goraczko, M., Zhao, F. (2008) Tiny Web Services: Design and Implementation of Interoperable and Evolvable Sensor Networks, Microsoft Research, ACM 978-1-59593-990-6/08/11, North Carolina 2008

Schaltegger, S., Herzig, C., Kleiber, O, Klinke, T., Müller, J. (2007) Nachhaltigkeitsmanagement in Unternehmen - von der Idee zur Praxis: Managementansätze zur Umsetzung von Corporate Social Responsibility und Corporate Sustainability, Forschungsbericht des Bundesministeriums für Umwelt, Naturschutz und Reaktorsicherheit, 2007

Young, T., Burton, M.P. (1992) Agricultural sustainability: definition and implications for agricultural and trade policy, Rome 1992

Web:

EMAS (2011) Umweltmanagementsystem, http://www.emas.de/ueber-emas/umweltmanagement/, Page view on 27.09.2011

Financial Times Lexicon (2011) Financial Times Lexicon, definition of psychic income, http://lexicon.ft.com/Term?term=psychic-income, Page view on 05.08.2011

Golem (2011) SAP holt sich Know-how für 3D-Visualisierung, http://www.heise.de/newsticker/meldung/SAP-holt-sich-Know-how-fuer-3D-Visualisierung-1338361.html, Page view on 07.09.2011

ISO 14000 (2011) ISO 14000 essentials, http://www.iso.org/iso/iso_14000_essentials, Page view on 27.09.2011

ISO 26000 (2011) ISO 26000, http://www.iso.org/iso/iso_catalogue/management_and_leadership_standards/social_responsibility/sr_discovering_iso26000.htm, Page view on 17.09.20011

Reh, F.J. (2011) Key Performance Indicators – How an organization defines and measures progress toward its goals, http://management.about.com/cs/generalmanagement/a/keyperfindic.htm, Page view on 27.07.2011